MUMMY
SECRETS OF THE TOMB

John H. Taylor

VMFA
VIRGINIA MUSEUM OF FINE ARTS

The Banner Exhibition Program at the Virginia Museum of Fine Arts is made possible by the Julia Louise Reynolds Fund.

The exhibition, *Mummy: Secrets of the Tomb*, is generously supported by the Lettie Pate Whitehead Evans Exhibition Endowment.

New American edition published in 2011
by Virginia Museum of Fine Arts
200 N. Boulevard, Richmond, Virginia 23220

www.vmfa.museum

Library of Congress Cataloguing-in-Publication Data available

ISBN: 978-0-917046-98-8

Designed by Price Watkins
Printed in China by C&C Offset Printing Co. Ltd

The papers used in this book are recyclable products and the manufacturing processes are expected to conform to the environmental regulations of the country of origin.

The vast majority of the objects illustrated in this book are from the collection of the British Museum. Further information about the collection can be found on the museum website at britishmuseum.org.
For online tours of the Egyptian galleries visit:
britishmuseum.org/explore/online_tours.aspx

Front cover: Lid of Nesperennub's painted wooden coffin. Thebes, *c.*1069–715 BC. L. 173 cm. EA 30720. © The Trustees of the British Museum.
Back cover: The mummy of Nesperennub, with amulets and funerary trappings *in situ.* © The Trustees of the British Museum.

CONTENTS

FOREWORD

ONE of the first questions I was asked after becoming director of the Virginia Museum of Fine Arts was, "Will the mummy ever go on display again?" An encounter with *Tjeby*, VMFA's mummy, is an important childhood memory for many. For several years prior to my arrival the VMFA mummy had been in storage, victim to differing opinions about the appropriateness of displaying human remains. However, the redesign of our Egyptian galleries in 2011 allowed an opportunity to reconsider and re-contextualize the display and present *Tjeby* in a more sensitive manner.

With this local history in mind we are delighted to have the opportunity to host an exhibition that explores the subject of mummies in detail and draws on one of the world's greatest collections of Egyptian art to tell that story. The mysteries of ancient Egypt and, in particular, the rituals and beliefs surrounding death and the afterlife continue to exert endless fascination for every generation. Since its foundation the British Museum has been at the forefront of archaeological and scientific exploration in Egypt and is a treasure house of some of the greatest artifacts uncovered. The Museum's multiyear analysis of the mummy of the priest Nesperennub, which uncovered new objects as well as the mummy itself, is one of the most remarkable uses of state-of-the-art scanning technology to date. The resulting 3D film allows us to travel through millennia and enter into the life and death of an Egyptian priest. I believe every visitor will be thrilled by the experience.

Many are involved with an exhibition of this scope, but I would like to single out a few people in particular. At the British Museum Neil MacGregor, Director, Dr. John Taylor, Assistant Keeper, Ancient Egypt and curator of the exhibition, and Amanda Mayne, International Touring Exhibitions Manager, displayed great generosity and flexibility when helping us create a final checklist of objects for this unique North American presentation of the exhibition. At VMFA the project team consisted of Robin Nicholson, Deputy Director for Art and Education; Dr. Peter Schertz, Jack and Mary Ann Frable Curator of Ancient Art; and Aiesha Halstead, Manager of Exhibitions. The logistics of bringing these incredible objects to Virginia were deftly managed by Senior Assistant Registrar, Karen Daly, and the dramatic and sensitive exhibition design was executed by Head of Design, Doug Fisher. Finally the rich educational programming and engaging complementary exhibition on the Rosetta Stone and the history of writing were the work of Della Watkins, Chief Educator.

OPPOSITE The lid of Nesperennub's painted wooden coffin. Thebes, c.1069–715 BC. H. 192 cm. British Museum EA 30720.

Alex Nyerges
Director
Virginia Museum of Fine Arts

INTRODUCTION

EGYPTIAN mummies are perennially popular with visitors to museums – but what is their relevance in the twenty-first century? What can we learn from the study of these ancient remains?

Mummies are an unparalleled source of scientific data, addressing a host of questions about life in one of the most highly-developed societies of the ancient world. Although the ancient Egyptians left many written records, these tell only part of the story, and researchers rely heavily on human remains to complete the picture. These throw light on many important issues about which the inscriptions are often silent: physical anthropology, family relationships, life expectancy, nutrition and health, disease and the causes of death. They also of course provide a unique insight into the fascinating and complex processes of mummification; including not only the artificial preservation of the corpse, but also the ritual elements which played such an important part: the placing of amulets, the putting on of wrappings and the equipping of the body with religious texts and images.

For many years, the only way to extract this data from Egyptian mummies was to unwrap them – a process both destructive and irreversible. Then, the advent of modern non-invasive imaging techniques – X-rays and Computerized Tomography (CT) scanning – made it possible to look inside a mummy without disturbing the wrappings in any way. Now this technology has advanced still further. Thanks to the latest computer-generated images, we are able to perform a 'virtual unwrapping' of a mummy and to embark on a journey within the body, visualizing every feature and amulet in 3D. This technology has been applied to the mummy of the priest Nesperennub. His beautifully painted mummy-case has been one of the British Museum's treasured exhibits for over a hundred years. It has never been opened since it was sealed up by embalmers on the West Bank at Thebes shortly before he was buried, but now after 2,800 years technology has unlocked its secrets. The wealth of images that have been captured in this way have already proved valuable to researchers, and will bring museum visitors face to face with a man from the remote past in a unique and fascinating way.

This book takes the reader on a journey of discovery, gathering information about Nesperennub from a variety of sources. First, his place in history and his role in Egyptian society are pieced together from the inscriptions – the formal record of his life which was intended for posterity. Then the 3D technology makes it possible to enter the mummy-case and to explore the body, collecting data about Nesperennub as a person, seeing his face, assessing his health, and looking over the shoulders of the embalmers as they prepared him for eternal life.

OPPOSITE The mummy of Nesperennub, with amulets and funerary trappings *in situ*.

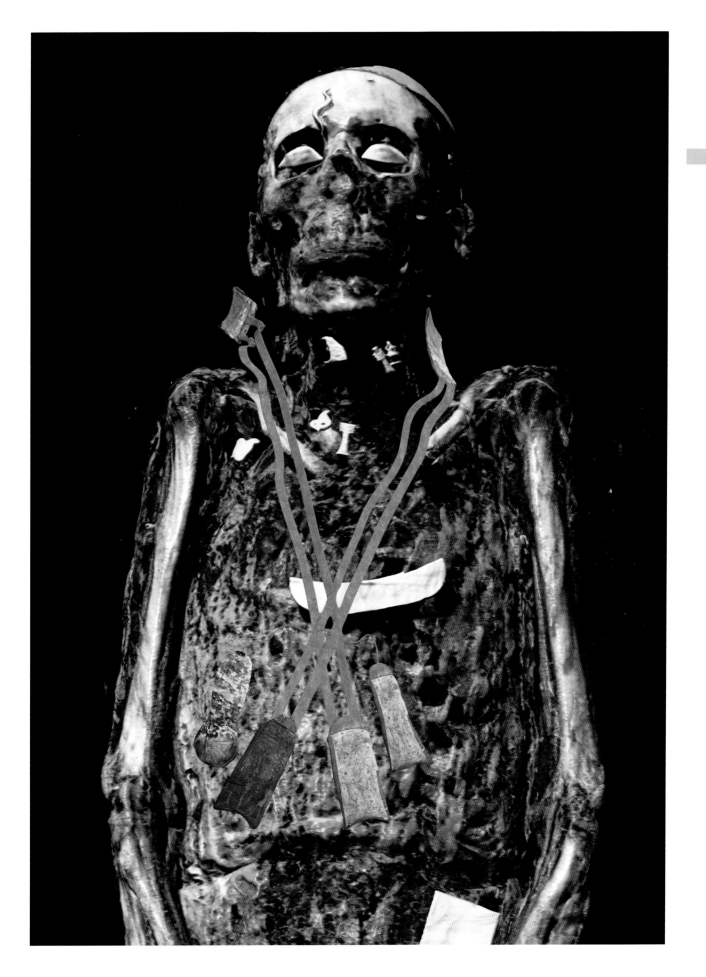

THE DISCOVERY OF NESPERENNUB

ABOVE E.A. Wallis Budge (1857–1934).

LEFT The mummy of Nesperennub in its cartonnage case. Thebes, 1069–715 BC. H. 173 cm. British Museum EA 30720.

NESPERENNUB's body, enclosed in a cartonnage (linen and plaster) case and a wooden coffin, is an excellent specimen of Egyptian mummification practices in the Twenty-second and Twenty-third Dynasties (c.945–715 BC). It was discovered at Luxor, the site of the ancient city of Thebes, in the 1890s and bought by E.A. Wallis Budge on one of his regular visits to Egypt to collect antiquities for the British Museum. The mummy and its cases were sent to England by the shipping company Moss of Alexandria in 1899.

Nesperennub's burial had probably been found by local diggers in a tomb on the West Bank at Thebes, but Budge left no record of its exact location. It is unlikely that he was ever shown the find *in situ*; the local dealers who acted as suppliers of antiquities were often reticent about revealing their sources. During the ninth and eighth centuries BC, when Nesperennub lived, many of the citizens of Thebes were buried in the sepulchres of officials of the New Kingdom (c.1550–1069 BC) – the 'tombs of the nobles', whose brilliantly painted chapels in the cliffs facing the Nile are among the spots most visited by today's tourists.

Although many of these tombs were then five, six or seven centuries old, they were still in use, ownership often passing from one family to another. Mummies were interred either in the burial chambers of the original occupants of the tombs, or at the bottom of shafts newly cut below the courtyards or chapels. Sometimes mummies were placed in the painted chapel itself, which was then sealed up. Alternatively, entirely new tombs were being constructed within the enclosures of temples along the edge of the Nile floodplain. But burials found there are generally less well-preserved than those from the New Kingdom tombs higher up in the cliffs; the excellent preservation of Nesperennub's coffins may indicate that he was interred in one of these older tombs.

Together with Nesperennub's mummy, the British Museum also purchased another coffin, inscribed for a man named Ankhefenkhons. Budge identified this man as the father of Nesperennub, and the inscriptions on their coffins support this. It is probable, then, that the burial place, wherever it was, accommodated several members

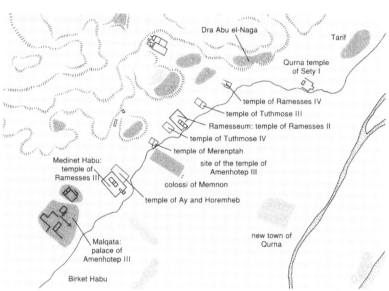

Dra Abu el-Naga

Tarif

Qurna temple of Sety I

temple of Ramesses IV

temple of Tuthmose III

Ramesseum: temple of Ramesses II

temple of Tuthmose IV

temple of Merenptah

site of the temple of Amenhotep III

Medinet Habu: temple of Ramesses III

colossi of Memnon

temple of Ay and Horemheb

new town of Qurna

Malqata: palace of Amenhotep III

Birket Habu

of the same family. The mummy of Ankhefenkhons has not come to light, but in the nineteenth century objects that were found together were frequently offered for sale to different collectors, so the body might have been purchased by someone other than Budge. This is all the more likely because between 1899 and 1905 the American Egyptologist George Reisner, acting on behalf of Phoebe Apperson Hearst, bought another set of coffins which probably came from the same family tomb. These are now in the Hearst Museum of Anthropology at the University of California, Berkeley. The inscriptions identify the owner as the lady Neskhonspakhered, and she is described as the wife of Nesperennub, son of Ankhefenkhons. The husband is credited with the same priestly titles as the British Museum's Nesperennub, and any doubt that Neskhonspakhered was married to him is dispelled at a glance, as both husband and wife have matching coffins, clearly made and painted by the same craftsmen. They must have been ordered at around the same time. Unfortunately, the mummy of Neskhonspakhered is also missing; perhaps it was sold to another collector, or left behind in Egypt.

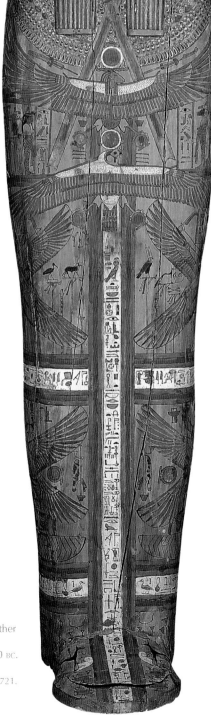

Wooden coffin of Ankhefenkhons, father of Nesperennub. Thebes, c.850–800 BC. H. 180 cm. British Museum EA 30721.

EGYPT IN THE LIBYAN PERIOD

THE structure of society that arose in Egypt under the rule of the pharaohs endured for over 3,000 years. Its phases of greatest prosperity – the Old Kingdom, Middle Kingdom, New Kingdom and Late Period – were distinguished by a strong government, a healthy economy and a dominant influence on the world stage. In each of these periods, which lasted from 200 to 500 years, Egypt projected a well-defined view of itself, ideally as a unified land, with a centralized authority under a hereditary monarchy. Each phase left highly visible and impressive monuments. These periods were separated by times of relative weakness, and it was in one of these, between c.1069 and 664 BC, that Nesperennub lived. It is now known as the Third Intermediate Period. The priest Manetho, who compiled the first comprehensive history of Egypt in the third century BC, recognized five lines of kings during this period, which he numbered as the Twenty-first to Twenty-fifth Dynasties. Although this terminology is still used by Egyptologists, the true political situation in Egypt was more complex than this sequential numbering suggests.

During the later years of the New Kingdom (c.1550–1069 BC) Egypt had been forced to defend her borders against the incursions of Libyan tribes from the western desert fringes. Although a violent conquest was avoided, Libyans had been allowed to settle in Egypt – many of them as garrison troops in fortresses. Peaceful migration into the western Nile Delta increased their numbers, and over time some Libyans rose to high status. As the state system weakened under economic pressures, the Libyan chiefs

Limestone stela showing God's Wife of Amun Ankhnesneferibre offering sistra to the deity. Her Chief Steward, Sheshonq, stands behind her. Thebes, 26th Dynasty, c.575 BC. H. 54 cm. British Museum EA 835.

King Pimay, one of the rulers who was based at Tanis in the Delta, kneels to present offerings to a deity. Bronze. Egypt, 22nd Dynasty, c.770 BC. H. 30 cm. British Museum EA 32747.

succeeded in gaining the highest posts, ultimately becoming pharaohs themselves. Most of the rulers of Egypt in the Twenty-first to Twenty-fourth Dynasties were of Libyan ancestry. They became culturally assimilated, at least outwardly, adopting Egyptian customs and worshipping Egyptian gods, but they allowed the centralized state to gradually disintegrate and the country became politically fragmented. Hence the Twenty-second to Twenty-fifth Dynasties were all to some degree contemporaneous, and besides these royal lines there were many other centres of power, some of them under the authority of Chiefs of the Ma (Meshwesh), a Libyan tribe.

At the time in which Nesperennub lived, the senior royal line, the Twenty-second Dynasty, ruled from Tanis in the eastern Delta, but the territory controlled by these pharaohs had shrunk over the years as local rulers in various parts of Egypt became virtually independent. By the eighth century BC, the country had become a patchwork of

Limestone lintel. Ankhefenmut, a scribe and priest of the god Ptah, holding a feather fan, adores the royal titulary of King Siamun. Memphis, 21st Dynasty, c.978–959 BC. L. 219 cm.
British Museum EA 1470 (Donated by the Egyptian Research Account).

principalities (sovereign states). Thebes, long the centre of the cult of Amun-Ra, chief state god of Egypt, was the focus of one of these principalities. The powerful officials there resisted the imposition of authority from the north, and periods of civil war had even occurred, with rival factions competing for control. The post of high priest of Amun was of key importance and became the focus of bitter conflict. During the late ninth century BC, Prince Osorkon, son of King Takelot II, waged a long war against a faction at Thebes who disputed his claim to the post of high priest of Amun. The conflict swayed both ways, and Osorkon used ruthless means including public executions to impose his authority. He seems ultimately to have triumphed and to have been recognized not only as high priest but also as King Osorkon III. His line, the Twenty-third Dynasty, shared power in Egypt with the Twenty-second Dynasty and other chiefdoms, and his sphere of influence was probably restricted to Thebes and the Upper Egyptian cities of Hermopolis and Heracleopolis. Nesperennub may have witnessed some of the disturbing events of these times. He probably lived during the twenty-eight-year reign of Osorkon III (c.780 BC), since the inscription of his son Nebetkheper (p. 14) was carved in the shorter reign of the next pharaoh, Takelot III.

In the decades that followed, the political situation changed again. Towards the end of the eighth century BC a new stronger power arose in Kush (Nubia), whose rulers invaded Egypt and took control of the entire country. Although this line, the Twenty-fifth Dynasty, did not eradicate the principalities, they assumed the role of overlords and succeeded in imposing greater unity and cohesion on the land. At Thebes supreme religious authority was removed from the high priest and given to a princess of the royal house, henceforth known as the God's Wife of Amun or Divine Adoratress. She did not marry but adopted another princess as her successor, thus avoiding disputes over hereditary access to the post.

Scene carved on a block from the granite gateway of King Osorkon II, showing the pharaoh seated during the Sed or festival of royal renewal. Bubastis, 22nd Dynasty, c.874–850 BC. L. 168 cm.
British Museum EA 1105 (Donated by the Egyptian Exploration Fund).

GODS AND TEMPLES

THE hieroglyphic inscriptions on the coffins of Nesperennub and his family provide basic information which enable us to locate him in time and place. Typically, this data occurs in the context of standardized religious formulae, and gives us only Nesperennub's official titles and the names of his relatives. Nothing is disclosed about the personalities of the people concerned, their lifespans, or anything touching on the times in which they lived.

The inscription on the lid of Nesperennub's wooden coffin reads: An offering which the king gives to Ra-Horakhty-Atum, the lord of the two lands and of Heliopolis, [to] Ptah-Sokar-Osiris, the lord of the shetayet-shrine, [and to] Wennefer, the ruler of eternity, [in order that they] might give life, prosperity and health to the Beloved of the God, the Opener of the Doors of Heaven in Karnak, the Libationer of Khons of Benenet, Nesper[en]nub, son of the like-titled Ankhefenkhons, true of voice.

The text on the front of the cartonnage case provides much the same information in an abbreviated form: An offering which the king gives to Osiris, so that he might give life to the Beloved of the God, the Libationer of Khons of Benenet, Nesperennub, son of the like-titled Ankhefenkhons, true of voice.

These inscriptions reveal that Nesperennub and his father worked in the great religious complex of Karnak, the cult-centre of the god Amun-Ra. This deity was the supreme god of the Egyptian state, and was the senior

ABOVE Reconstruction of the city of Thebes, c.1100 BC, looking from the temples of Karnak towards the tombs on the west bank of the Nile.

RIGHT Name and titles of Nesperennub, from his cartonnage mummy-case (p. 8). British Museum EA 30720.

FAR RIGHT Inscription on the lid of the outer, wooden coffin of Nesperennub. L. 192 cm. British Museum EA 30720.

figure of a 'holy family', the other members of which were the goddess Mut, wife of Amun-Ra, and the god Khons, their son. The father and mother deities each had a complete temple-complex of their own at Karnak. The temple of Khons (called Benenet by the ancient Egyptians) was situated in the south-west corner of the complex of Amun-Ra.

Khons was a very ancient deity who was associated with the moon. His name, which means 'wanderer', refers to the moon's passage across the night sky, and he is usually depicted wearing a lunar disc and crescent as his headdress. Khons is often shown with the head of a falcon, but when his role as the child of Amun and Mut is emphasized he usually appears in fully human form, shaven-headed except for a curled sidelock and often holding one finger to his lips – both standard conventions used by Egyptian artists to represent a child.

Nesperennub may have served in the temple of Amun-Ra, but it appears that he was mainly associated with the cult of Khons. His links with that priesthood are further emphasized by an inscription found on the roof-terrace of the temple of Khons (p. 14). This text was carved for a man named Nebetkheper, who was the son of Nesperennub. The inscription is dated to the seventh year of the reign of Takelot III of the Twenty-third Dynasty (c.750 BC). The inscription supplements the data from the coffins by recording other titles held by Nesperennub (p. 18). It also includes a long pedigree, listing many of his ancestors; this information can be compared with the genealogical data from the coffin of his father Ankhefenkhons (pp. 20–1). All of this written evidence makes clear that Nesperennub was a man of high status and a member of a clan which had wielded influence at Thebes for many years.

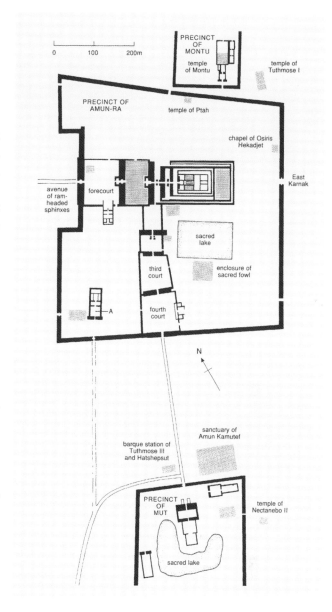

Plan of the temples of Karnak. A = temple of Khons.

The temple of Amun-Ra at Karnak, looking north-west across the Sacred Lake.

NESPERENNUB THE PRIEST

WE know that Nesperennub belonged to a long-established family of priests. In earlier periods, priestly duties were performed by ordinary citizens for a specified time, but from the New Kingdom (c.1550–1069 BC) it was customary for people to serve as 'full-time' priests. The roles of the priests became diversified. Each office carried a stipend and brought with it specific duties – though in practice these were rarely onerous. Posts were hereditary, and it was common for particular families to serve in the same temple for many generations. At the same time, an individual could 'collect' offices, entitling him to carry out a variety of duties in different temples. The more junior priests worked on a shift-basis, rotating on and off duty in groups. While their term of office lasted, they were obliged to observe regulations relating to purity: they had to bathe in the temple lake, have their heads shaved, abstain from sexual contacts and follow dietary restrictions and a dress code.

Some priestly titles were indications of rank. This perhaps applies to Nesperennub's 'Beloved of the God', a common title of Theban

Entrance to the temple of Khons at Karnak.

BELOW LEFT Bronze statuette of the god Khons. The curled sidelock and the position of the right hand, with finger to lip, signify his youthfulness. On his head is the moon in two forms, full disc and crescent, and above that a crown adorned with ram's horns and ostrich feathers. Egypt, Late Period, c.600 BC. H. 22. British Museum EA 35418.

BELOW Hieroglyphic inscription from the roof-terrace of the temple of Khons. Dated to the seventh year of the reign of King Takelot III (c.750 BC), it mentions Nesperennub and several members of his family.
After a copy by Georges Daressy.

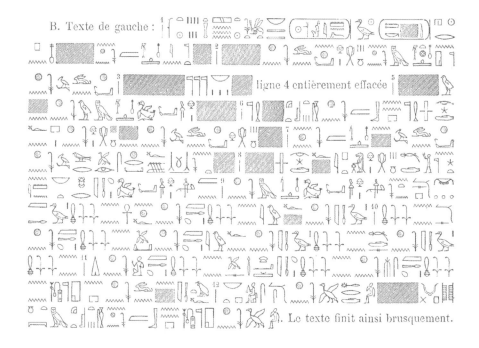

B. Texte de gauche :

ligne 4 entièrement effacée

Le texte finit ainsi brusquement.

ABOVE A shaven-headed priest burning incense and making an offering before the god Osiris. Painting on a wooden box for shabti-figures (funerary statuettes). Egypt, 19th or 20th Dynasty, c.1295–1069 BC. H. 26 cm. British Museum EA 35648.

RIGHT Bronze statue of a priest named Khonsirdis. He is shaven-headed and wears a leopard-skin over his linen garment – a traditional mark of priestly status. In his hands he originally held a statuette of a deity, only the plinth of which remains. Egypt, early 26th Dynasty, c.6664–610 BC. H. 40 cm. British Museum EA 14466 (Donated by Dr. Harry Reginald Holland Hall).

priests at the time, but one which does not seem to have carried clearly-defined duties. Others were connected to the daily ritual which was carried out in every temple. The temple served as an earthly home for the god, whose spirit was believed to animate the 'cult image' – a statue made of precious metal, which was kept in the sanctuary, or holy-of-holies. Every day, the shrine containing the god's image was opened. It was purified and clothed and nourishment was offered to it. Nesperennub's title 'Opener of the Doors of Heaven' indicates that he performed part of this ritual: his job was to open the doors of the shrine. The revelation of the god each morning

A miniature shrine in copper alloy, containing a figure of the god Amun-Ra. A deeply-carved inscription on the base allowed the shrine to be used as a seal. The object reproduces the appearance of larger shrines which were installed in the sanctuaries of temples. It bears the name of Thutemhat, a local king of the 23rd Dynasty, c.800–750 BC. H. (figure) 8 cm, H. (shrine) 11 cm. British Museum EA 11015.

was likened to the rising of the sun into the sky at dawn – a moment that for the Egyptians symbolized the renewal of all life and creation. Other priests then burned incense and performed the god's toilet and feeding. This part of the ritual involved the pouring of libations to purify the god's dwelling and his meal. The coffin inscriptions show that here too Nesperennub played his role, sprinkling water from a tall libation-jar over the offering table in front of the cult-statue.

The inscription from the Karnak temple gives Nesperennub the title 'Fan-bearer on the right hand of Khons'. This role would be performed at religious festivals at specified times of the year. The image of Khons, mounted on a miniature barque (boat), would be brought out of his temple and carried in procession on the shoulders of priests. Others would carry fans to create a breeze and drive away flies. These processions were rare opportunities for the ordinary citizens of Thebes to approach closely to the gods. On such occasions people could stand before the deity and ask him or her to give divine judgement in some dispute; the god thus acted as an oracle. Records of some of these incidents that took place at Thebes have survived. In some cases the deity is asked to decide whether or not a defendant is guilty of theft; in others he/she is petitioned to sanction the appointment of a person to a post in the temple hierarchy. In all of these consultations the god's decision was conveyed by some distinctive movement of the barque in which his image sat, carried by the priests.

In the Old and Middle Kingdoms it was not generally possible for an ordinary individual to approach the

RIGHT Granite statue of the vizier Nespekashuty, holding a large sistrum decorated with the head of the goddess Hathor. Egypt, 26th Dynasty, c.650 BC. H. 74 cm. British Museum EA 1125 (Donated by Government of the British Protectorate of Egypt).

BELOW Mummified cat with face modelled in linen. Egypt, Roman Period, after 30 BC. H. 46 cm. British Museum EA 55614 (Donated by W. A. Norman).

gods directly in this way. This kind of personal relationship with a divine being developed throughout the New Kingdom, and during the Libyan Period means of access to the gods increased. It was at about this time that there began a great increase in the production of votive offerings – items which a person presented to the god at his or her temple, often in the hope that a prayer or request would be conveyed to the deity along with the offering. Copper alloy statuettes were among the commonest of these votives. These are small images of the deity, sometimes bearing a short inscription on the base, requesting the god to 'give life' to the dedicator. The production of high quality cast metal statuary was a distinctive feature of this period; some of the images represent the dedicator himself.

Another means of communicating with the gods was via the presentation of mummified animals. Many deities were particularly associated with a specific creature: cats for the goddess Bastet, crocodiles for Sobek, ibises for Thoth, and many others. During the first millennium BC and even into the Roman period many thousands of these animals and birds were mummified to be offered to the deity at religious festivals. These mummies served as another type of votive image, and conveyed the petitioner's prayer to the deity. They were afterwards buried in special necropoleis, where millions of specimens have been found. Radiography of the mummies indicates that the animals were often killed; many cats are found to have suffered death from a broken neck or a blow to the head.

SERVING THE KING

18

PRIESTLY duties would not occupy all of Nesperennub's time. Many priests also held secular offices alongside their religious functions. These were often posts in the administration or even in the army. Nesperennub was no exception, but because coffins often carried predominantly religious titles it is only from the Karnak inscription (p. 14) that we learn that he was 'Fan-bearer on the right hand of the king'. The fanbearers attended on the king on formal occasions and in processions. Despite its rather menial sound, it was a privileged position. Fanbearers had direct access to the pharaoh, and might be able to exert an influence over royal policy.

RIGHT Figure of the Chief Steward Sheshonq from the stela illustrated on p. 10. The small ostrich-feather fan he carries is similar to those which royal fan-bearers would have held. British Museum EA 835.

BELOW Limestone stela of the priest Ankhefenmut. The long inscription records his ancestry; in the last line is the name of King Takelot III, from whom he claimed descent. 26th Dynasty, c.664–525 BC. H. 37 cm. British Museum EA 74892 (Donated by Croydon Museum Service).

OPPOSITE Upper part of a calcite statue of an unidentified pharaoh of the 30th Dynasty or early Ptolemaic period, 4th–3rd century BC. H. 75 cm. British Museum EA 941 (Donated by Queen Victoria).

Although the king in question is not named the date of the inscription indicates that it may have been the long-lived Osorkon III, or perhaps his son and successor Takelot III, both of whom had close connections with Thebes. These rulers left their mark at Karnak and Hermopolis and in the Dakhleh Oasis, where minor building works and inscribed stelae have been found, but little is known of their other activities.

In earlier phases of Egyptian history, especially the New Kingdom, the king held supreme authority over the administration, religion and the army. As chief priest of every deity he was the sole intermediary between men and the gods, and was considered the living incarnation of the god Horus, a status to be inherited by his successor (ideally his son). During the Libyan Period, several pharaohs ruled simultaneously and every one claimed to be the living Horus. Each would have a court of officials, traditionally headed by the *tjaty* (vizier, or prime minister of state). These men were often members of influential families, and to secure their allegiance the Libyan pharaohs sometimes gave their daughters to them in marriage. Descendants of such marriages recorded their royal ancestry for posterity (left).

NESPERENNUB'S FAMILY

20

F AMILY ties were of great importance in the everyday lives of the ancient Egyptians. Marriage, with the procreation of many children, was the aspiration of most people. Property – whether land, movable goods or lucrative offices – was passed from generation to generation, and children were expected in their turn to provide for the burial and funerary cult of their dead parents. The recording of genealogies helped to establish hereditary claims to property on earth and to priestly or official titles.

From the Karnak inscription (p. 14) and from the coffins of Nesperennub, his father Ankhefenkhons and his wife Neskhonspakhered, an extensive genealogy can be reconstructed. This shows that the family had been attached to the cult of Khons for centuries, and that their titles had been passed from father to son for many generations. As a sign of their special devotion to the god they served, most of these individuals were given names which

Cartonnage mummy-case of Neskhonspakhered, wife of Nesperennub. This case is decorated in a style similar to that of Nesperennub himself. Both husband and wife also possessed almost identical outer wooden coffins which were probably made in the same craftsmen's workshop. Thebes, 22nd Dynasty. H. 173 cm. Phoebe A. Hearst Museum, Berkeley, California, 6-19929.

Nesperennub's family-tree, as reconstructed from two different sources:
A, inscription from the temple of Khons at Karnak;
B, inscriptions on the coffins of Nesperennub, his father Ankhefenkhons and his wife Neskhonspakhered

A. GENEALOGY FROM KARNAK INSCRIPTION	B. GENEALOGY FROM INSCRIPTION ON COFFINS
WENEN ...	
KHONSMOSE	
PAESAAKHAU	
DIKHONS	
SHEDSUKI IONS	
IUFENKHONS	IUFENKHONS
PADIKHONS	PADIKHONS
NESKHONS	SHEDSUKHONS
IUFENKHONS	IUFFNKHONS
ANKHEFENKHONS KHONSPAKHERED	ANKHEFENKHONS
NESPERENNUB = NESKHONSPAKHERED	NESPERENNUB = NESKHONSPAKHERED
NEBETKHEPER	

Funerary pair statue of Mahu (right) and his wife Duat, whose arm is outstretched to embrace her husband. The group exemplifies the importance of the marital ties, which were expected to persist after death. Egypt, mid to late 18th Dynasty, c.1350–1300 BC. Limestone, H. 63 cm. British Museum EA 460.

incorporated that of Khons himself. The sources are in complete agreement about the sequence of names except at one point; Nesperennub's great-grandfather is named in the coffin texts as Shedsukhons, but in the Karnak inscription he is called Neskhons. These two names could easily be confused when written in hieroglyphs or in hieratic script. There are two possible explanations. As this section of the Karnak inscription is heavily damaged, the name may simply have been misread by Georges Daressy, the French Egyptologist who copied and published it in the 1890s. Alternatively, one of the ancient scribes who wrote the original texts may himself have made a mistake; such confusions occur quite often in repetitive genealogical texts.

Nesperennub's wife came from another family which held office in the same temple. Her name, Neskhonspakhered, means 'She who belongs to Khons the Child', and her father was a Libation-priest of Khons, as well as a shrine-opener and temple scribe. This intermarriage of the son and daughter of two professional colleagues is an indication of the close-knit world of the priests, and the influence of the temple on their daily lives.

It was expected that a married couple would have children, who would in due course support and care for their parents in their old age. In the case of Nesperennub only one child – Nebetkheper – is known. There may have been others, of whom no record has been found.

DEATH, BURIAL AND AFTERLIFE

A STRONG belief in the afterlife was one of the defining elements of ancient Egyptian culture. For them death was not the end of existence, but was a threshold or transition to another phase of life. In many of their writings a contrast was drawn between the brevity of human life and the everlasting afterlife: 'The time one spends on earth is but a dream, but "Welcome, safe and sound!" is said to the one who has reached the West.' Examination of human remains confirms that life expectancy was low; those who survived the dangers of childhood could not expect to live much beyond thirty years. This attitude is reflected in the abodes the Egyptians made for the living and the dead. Earthly houses (even royal palaces) were for temporary occupation only, and were built of perishable materials – mud brick, wood, reed – whereas tombs were designed to last for eternity and so, where possible, were constructed of stone. Naturally such monuments were costly to produce, but proper preparation for the afterlife was viewed as a highly important matter, as the wisdom text known as the 'Instruction of Any' (c.1500 BC) records: 'Furnish your place in the valley of the dead. Place this before you as one of your concerns. When your envoy (of death) comes to fetch you, let him find you ready.'

The universe was explained in religious terms. It was dominated by natural cycles – the movements of the sun, moon and stars, the growth of plant life, the annual flooding of the Nile – and it was believed that these patterns were brought about by divine agency. Human life was also seen as cyclical and renewable. After passing through death one entered into a closer relationship with these eternal powers, dwelling in the realms of the gods, which were located in the sky and beneath the earth. Two deities in particular were believed to hold the key to eternal life: Ra, the sun god and creator of the universe, who travelled across the sky each day by boat and passed through the subterranean netherworld by night; and Osiris, the king of the dead, whose realm was the netherworld. Osiris, who had himself risen from death to eternal life, represented the ideal to which all Egyptians aspired; many of the elaborate funerary practices of the elite aimed to identify the deceased closely with Osiris in order to ensure that he/she too would live for ever.

Ancient Egyptian texts refer to the notion that a per-

Limestone stela of Neferabu. The lower scene shows the god Anubis embalming a corpse. Above, on the day of burial, four mummies undergo the ritual of the Opening of the Mouth. Probably from Deir el-Medina, 19th Dynasty, c.1250 BC. H. 63 cm. British Museum EA 305.

son was manifested through many different media. These included the physical body, the heart, the name and the shadow. Each person also possessed intangible 'spirits' called the *ka* and the *ba*. The *ka* is often interpreted as a kind of vital force, which was passed from parent to child; when depicted it is shown as an exact copy of the person, but the hieroglyphic sign for *ka*, a pair of upraised arms, conveys the notion of an embrace, signifying the transference of vital power from one individual to another. The *ba*, a more independent spirit, approaches more closely the modern concept of the personality (the word was equated with psyche by the Greeks). At the point of death the connection between these numerous aspects of the self was severed, and for life to resume that connection had to be re-established. This was the fundamental aim of much of the funerary practices of the Egyptians, a highly important element of which was the formal treatment of the dead body. Early burials show the importance that was

The mummy of Padiamenet, an official of the temple of Ra at Thebes. It is enclosed within a cartonnage case, similar to that of Nesperennub. 25th Dynasty, c.700 BC. L. 176 cm. British Museum EA 6682.

ABOVE Fragmentary tomb relief showing the gods Thoth and Horus pouring a life-giving libation of water over the deceased, the priest Nesmin, whose figure is missing. Limestone. Egypt, Late Period, 664–305 BC. L. 150 cm. British Museum EA 1235.

attached to protecting it to prevent its destruction. Natural preservation by the desiccating desert sand often aided in this, and this was succeeded by artificial procedures to frustrate the destructive processes of decomposition.

The first known attempts in Egypt to preserve the dead body by artificial methods date to around 3500 BC, at which date resin and linen wrappings were being applied to the surface of the corpse to help retain its physical integrity. The techniques steadily evolved over the next three millennia, reaching a peak of creativity and efficiency around 1000 BC. These procedures, now called mummification, varied also according to the amount one spent; by the fifth century BC the Greek historian Herodotus was able to report that three methods were available, ranging from the elaborate (and most expensive) to the simple (and cheapest). In all such treatments the basic aims were the same; by removing the fluid content and the perishable internal organs the corpse was purged of the foul-smelling

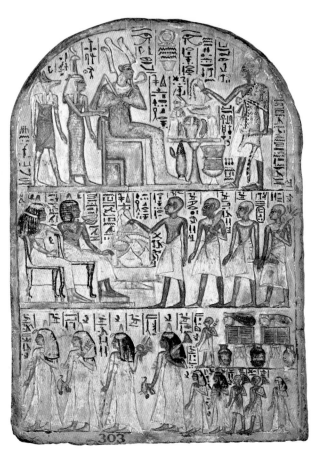

LEFT Limestone funerary stela of Qeh. At the top a priest makes offerings to Osiris, and below the dead man and his wife receive offerings from their sons and daughters. Abydos, early 19th century, c.1250 BC. H. 67 cm. British Museum EA 303.

BELOW Painted wooden model of a funerary boat carrying a mummy beneath a canopy. Thebes, 12th Dynasty, c.1850 BC. L. 78 cm. British Museum EA 9525.

products of decomposition, and by anointing it, packing, stuffing and applying cosmetic treatments it was reconstructed and fashioned into a new, divine body; one fit for eternal life among the gods.

No less important was the proper disposal of the body in a permanent resting place – the tomb, often referred to as the 'house of eternity'. From a very early date Egyptian tombs were located on the west bank of the Nile, the place where the sun set. The 'Beautiful West' became a circumlocution for the region to which the dead were believed to go. In earlier periods a kind of eternal life in the cemetery was envisaged, with the spirits of the dead dwelling in or near the tomb, but later the idea developed that the dead entered an eternal realm located in the sky and the netherworld, to which the tomb was the point of access. It was also the place of earthly contact between the living and the dead, for the dead were regarded as still part of the community, entities with whom contact could be maintained, at least as long as they survived as individuals in the memories of their relatives. An elaborate ritual service of the dead was maintained at the tomb.

The ritual process was an important means of transferring the individual from the earthly world to the eternal afterlife. It began immediately after death, when the body was taken from the house to undergo formal treatment to make it ready for burial. For a poor peasant this might mean a process of drying and wrapping, taking only a few days; for a wealthy person seventy days were traditionally set aside for the elaborate operations and chemical processes which are today known as mummification (pp. 40–53). This was itself a ritualized process; a late text known as the 'Ritual of Embalming' records the ceremonial aspects, such as the symbolic significance of different cloths which were to be used for wrapping the corpse, and how various amulets were to be placed. At the end of the seventy days the corpse, fully wrapped and enclosed

in a coffin, was returned to the family. The day of burial was the culmination of the ritual process on earth, when the mummy was conveyed in a procession to the tomb, crossing the Nile by boat to the west bank (even if only symbolically) and being hauled to the burial place by oxen. On this last journey, the dead person was accompanied by family, friends, colleagues and mourners. At the tomb further rites were performed under the rays of the shining sun, the most important of these acts being the 'Opening of the Mouth' ritual. By touching the mouth, eyes, ears and nose of the mummy's mask a priest symbolically opened those orifices. This act had strong connotations of rebirth, reawakening the dead, enabling them to feed, as a newborn baby, and giving back the power of speech, which would be needed in the divine realm which they were about to enter. The offering of the foreleg and heart, freshly cut from a living calf, also transferred the life force into the dead.

Care for the dead continued after the burial via a mortuary cult. The design of the tomb made special provision for this. In all but the simplest Egyptian tombs two main areas can be recognized: the burial chamber, which was subterranean and was sealed and inaccessible after the burial; and the chapel, located above ground, which remained open. Here the cult

ABOVE The 'Field of Reeds', an agricultural paradise in which the dead were believed to dwell. From the Papyrus of Kerqun. Thebes, Ptolemaic Period, c.250 BC. H. 40 cm. British Museum EA 9911.

BELOW A yellow marble headrest. Egypt, 6th Dynasty, c.2300 BC. H. 22 cm. British Museum EA 30413.

ABOVE Two shabti figures: a 'worker' holding hoes, wood, 18th Dynasty, c.1350 BC, H. 21 cm, and an 'overseer' holding a whip, faience, 21st Dynasty, c.1030 BC, H. 12 cm. British Museum EA 34134, 18588.

was performed; the focus of attention being a statue of the deceased, which was sometimes visible, and sometimes concealed in a hidden chamber. In tombs and chapels of the New Kingdom there were often group-statues representing husband and wife (p. 21), sometimes accompanied by other family members. The living relatives visited the chapel to recite a prayer for the well-being of their ancestors and to place food and drink on the offering table to nourish their *ka* spirits. This was traditionally the duty of the son. It was a service similar in concept and intent to the cult of the gods; their statues located in the sanctuaries of the temples received offerings every day, and through a reciprocal arrangement the gods would act benevolently towards men and the cosmic order would be maintained as it had at the 'first time', the moment of creation. In their tombs the dead – if well looked after – would themselves be well-disposed to the living, refraining from bringing misfortune and perhaps even providing supernatural help in times of difficulty.

Provisioning was an essential element of the care of the dead. Their *ka* spirits needed the basic staples of life – food, drink, clothing – but the offerings that their relatives brought to the tomb chapel were only tokens; eventually these supplies would fail. To perpetuate these benefits eternally they had recourse to the magical power that was believed to reside in word and image. Pictures of the items needed by the dead could be carved or painted on the walls of the tomb or the sides of the coffin to provide access to an unlimited supply; depictions of servants

Osiris presiding over the weighing of the heart of the dead man on a balance, to determine whether or not his conduct in life has rendered him deserving of admission to the realm of the blessed dead. Papyrus of Ankhwahibre. Probably from the Memphite necropolis. Late 26th Dynasty, c.550–525 BC. British Museum EA 10558,18.

baking bread, slaughtering oxen and weaving cloth – both in two- and three-dimensional form – fulfilled the same purpose. The words of the spell that called forth offerings were inscribed in the tomb as another way of eternalizing the ritual; they are often preceded by an address to living visitors to the tomb chapel, urging them to speak the words aloud.

Magic pervaded everyday life in ancient Egypt, being used to fight sickness and misfortune and to give protection in dangerous situations such as childbirth, and it is scarcely surprising that these supernatural powers were invoked to guide the dead through the difficult transition into eternal life. For the privileged and wealthy a range of magical texts was included in the tomb – written on the coffin or on long papyrus rolls. These latter contained magical spells from a repertoire that the ancient Egyptians called 'spells for coming forth by day', and which is today known as the 'Book of the Dead'. These texts endowed the deceased with special knowledge and powers that would be needed to make the challenging journey into the other realm.

The magical texts provided for the dead are revealing about the goals they were aiming at. In the earlier phases of Egyptian civilization the dead king was expected to as-

Lid (below) and base (left) of the granite sarcophagus of Nesisut, a priest of the temples of Memphis. Giza, 27th Dynasty, *c*.500 BC. L. 250 cm. British Museum EA 30.

cend to the sky to mingle with the gods, a destiny reserved for him alone or for a small and highly privileged circle of courtiers. In the New Kingdom and later periods the dead journeyed with the sun god by day or dwelt in a region called the Field of Reeds. This is illustrated in spell 110 of the 'Book of the Dead' as a landscape that includes much that is typical of that of Egypt – waterways, fields of corn, boats – where the blessed dead planted crops, harvested them to provide endless food, sailed in boats, mingled with the gods and were reunited with their families. It is a perfect version of Egypt, a homecoming without sickness, hunger or death. This idea of the afterlife as an agricultural society had a long history and other aspects of the earthly existence were also transposed into the beyond, including the notion that one could be subject to forced labour. But if this idea should seem incompatible with a life of leisured ease, magic again came to the rescue, for if the dead were summoned to labour in the fields of the beyond their tasks could be deputed to substitutes who would work on their behalf. These eternal workers were represented by the small mummy-shaped figurines called *shabtis*, which are found in many tombs.

Reaching the afterlife necessitated making proper material preparation, but there was also a moral dimension to be considered – the notion that destiny depended to some extent on personal character and the record of life on earth. The Egyptians had a clear notion of what constituted good and bad behaviour; principles of guidance are expressed through many wisdom texts, collections of maxims which advise the listener to act justly, to restrain greed, to avoid oppressing the weak, to relieve the needy, and to display loyalty to the king and respect to the gods. To observe these patterns of behaviour was to live according to Maat, the ideal state of cosmic order, which the gods maintained. In tomb inscriptions the owner often declares his good character by listing such virtues, from which we are to infer that he believed himself deserving of eternal life. Those who transgressed these codes would be denied this privilege. In the story of the Eloquent Peasant,

the righteous man will receive a proper funeral: 'He will be buried, and he will join the earth; but his name will not be erased on earth, he will be remembered because of his virtue.'

The fullest development of this idea is expressed in spell 125 of the 'Book of the Dead', where the deceased faces judgment before Osiris. His past life is scrutinized, he is required to declare himself free from all the sins that the gods abhor, and his heart is symbolically weighed in a balance. The heart here stands for the mind and memory of its owner, and it is also a crucial aspect of his existence; if lost or destroyed he himself will perish. A perfect balance between the heart and an image of Maat indicated a life spent in accordance with that principle, and the deceased was then declared *maa-kheru*, 'true of voice', and received into the realm of Osiris. If the heart was heavier than the feather of Maat, its owner was condemned and suffered the 'second death', his heart being swallowed by the monstrous 'Devourer' who crouched beside the scales.

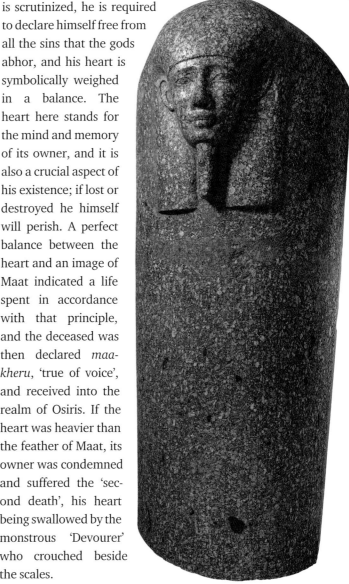

GATHERING DATA FROM MUMMIES

EGYPTOLOGISTS are fortunate in having an enormous amount of written evidence with which to reconstruct ancient Egyptian life and culture. The walls of tombs and temples were covered with hieroglyphic inscriptions, while rolls of papyrus, preserved almost pristine by the dry climate, contain often lengthy texts written in ink. But most of these writings are formal in character. Temple inscriptions and funerary texts reflect a stable and perfect world, in which all was controlled according to Maat, the ideal state of order.

The day to day realities were different. The Egyptians constantly battled natural and socio-political problems – famine and disease, economic stress and civil unrest. Such things did not fit with the concept of Maat, and mention of them is usually excluded from the formal inscriptions. Although some written sources throw light on these matters, they are rare and are unevenly distributed throughout the 3,000-year span of ancient Egyptian history.

The mummy of Nesperennub and its painted cases perfectly exemplify the discrepancies between the historian's sources. The mummiform coffins present us with idealized images of their occupant as young, handsome and healthy. The inscriptions proclaim his probity on earth through official titles indicating status and responsibility, and the paintings are reassuring indications that all will go well for him in the hereafter. The mummy within the coffins reveals much that is not expressed elsewhere, about physical anthropology, life expectancy, nutrition, health, disease, manner of death, and mummification processes – the realities of existence, which often could not be fully controlled and may have been far from the ideal. It is through examining the human remains that personal stories of life in the society of ancient Egypt can be revealed.

For many years, the only way to extract information from mummies was to unwrap them. In the early nineteenth century, mummy 'unrollings' were often dramatic performances, carried out before fee-paying audiences drawn from the fashionable elements of European society. Although there was some gain in knowledge, invasive

ABOVE Margaret Murray (1863–1963) and her team at the unwrapping of the mummy of one of the 'Two Brothers' at Manchester, 1908. Although this investigation was ahead of its time in pioneering a multi-disciplinary approach, the destructive effect of unwrapping is clearly apparent.

BELOW Invitation to the 'unrolling' of an Egyptian mummy in London, 1850.

study had many disadvantages: irreversible damage to the body and wrappings, the loss of the context of all objects found within the bandages, and sometimes the complete destruction of the mummy. Once a mummy has been unwrapped, much of its value as a time capsule is lost for ever. The original assemblage of evidence cannot be revisited to answer any new questions that may arise.

Non-invasive imaging has transformed this picture. The potential of X-rays for investigating Egyptian mummies was realized as early as the 1890s, and hundreds

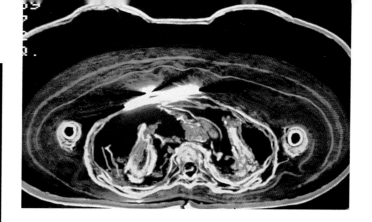

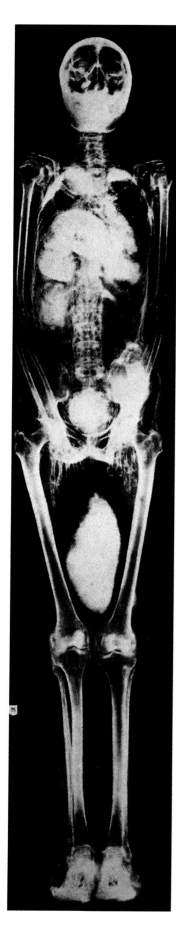

TOP CT image of the mummy of Tjentmutengebtiu from Thebes, c.900 BC. This cross-section through the cartonnage-case shows the layers of linen wrappings, the chest and arm-bones, and objects inside the body.

ABOVE Textile threads from a child mummy of the Roman Period, after 30 BC, viewed at very high magnification and high resolution using the technique of Environmental Scanning Electron Microscopy (ESEM). This is one of many highly refined imaging techniques which are increasingly being applied to the study of mummies.

LEFT Full-body radiograph of a Theban mummy of the 22nd Dynasty (945–715 BC), X-rayed as part of a general survey of mummies at the British Museum in the 1960s. Preserved internal organs and dense packing materials are visible within the chest and between the legs.

of mummies were X-rayed during the twentieth century. However, these images, created by projecting a single beam of radiation through the mummy, were not always clear. Anatomical structures and objects are superimposed on the X-ray plate, making them difficult to distinguish. The solidified resin and other dense materials inside mummies also impaired the clarity of the image. These problems were overcome by the development of CT (Computerized Tomography) scanning. The method involves passing X-ray beams through the body from different angles. This eliminates the difficulty of superimposed images and enables the data to be used with greater versatility. CT data can be displayed on a computer screen as a series of two-dimensional axial 'slices' through the body. This presents to the viewer everything within the object scanned. Different structures are distinguished according to their relative density on a scale from black (minimum density), through grey, to white (maximum density).

Features of specific and consistent densities (such as bone, ceramic or metal) can also be selected and displayed in the form of 3D images. Thus from the scanning of a mummy, a skull or individual bones can be isolated and viewed from any angle on a computer screen. Such reconstructions can even be animated to create a 'fly-through'. Thanks to this method, the unwrapping of mummies has become rare, and imaging technology continues to break new barriers.

IMAGING NESPERENNUB

ONVENTIONAL X-rays of the mummy of Nesperennub, made in the 1960s, had proved disappointing, with much of the finer detail obscured by opaque areas on the plates. A CT survey, carried out in 2000, provided much clearer images, and this was used in a collaboration between the British Museum and Silicon Graphics Inc (SGI) to create a full 3D volumetric dataset. This dataset formed the basis of the first version of the exhibition *Mummy: the Inside Story* (2004), a 3D experience for audiences, in which they were able to see the mummy 'virtually unwrapped' and explored on screen.

Since that time the quality of images that can be obtained by CT scanners has improved significantly, as has the technology by which such data can be visualized. In 2007 a new CT survey of Nesperennub was made when his mummy was scanned at University College Hospital, London, using a Siemens SOMATOM Sensation 64 scanner. This equipment employs a multi-slice technique, in which the body travels through the scanner while the source of radiation rotates, collecting data on different axial planes simultaneously. Cross-sectional images of the entire mummy were obtained at 0.6 mm intervals, a thickness which enables the individual slices to be reassembled into 3D images with a high degree of clarity. The viewer has the option to examine each cross-sectional slice separately, to create 3D reconstructions of any part of the body or to make a 'fly through' journey inside the mummy-case. The complete dataset contains a wealth of information, and software tools enable the investigator to adjust numerous parameters such as density and opacity to display different layers and structures, and to tease out fine detail buried deep within the body. A 'clipping plane', passed through any axis to remove sections of the dataset that the viewer does not wish to see, can act as a virtual scalpel, slicing cleanly through the body and exposing a cross-section of what is inside (pp. 33, 39, 40, 43). Artificial lighting casts shadows that help to interpret the shape of bones or objects.

The latest CT survey has enabled more accurate assessments to be made of some features of Nesperennub's mummy, in particular of the amulets placed beneath his

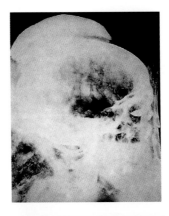

LEFT Conventional X-ray of the head of Nesperennub, made in the 1960s. The cloudy image shows only that artificial eyes are present and that there is a dense object on the top of the skull.

BELOW Cross-sectional CT slice, showing the contents of the cartonnage case, including the linen wrappings, the arm bones and spine and the contents of the chest cavity.

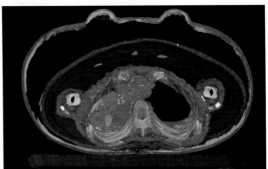

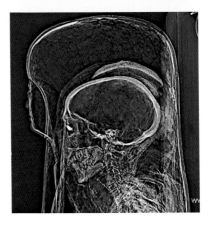

Lateral topogram, or preliminary CT film, showing the body of Nesperennub. The skull is positioned at a lower level than the face of the mummy-case with an empty space above. This indicates that the case was made to a standard size, rather than being built up around the mummy itself.

wrappings. Some of these, previously difficult to recognize, can now be identified with confidence (pp. 44–9). What had been thought to be rings on the fingers are now revealed as small strings of beads and tiny amulets (p. 49), while the leather bands that had been placed over the chest (seen only faintly in the earlier scans) now stand out with startling clarity.

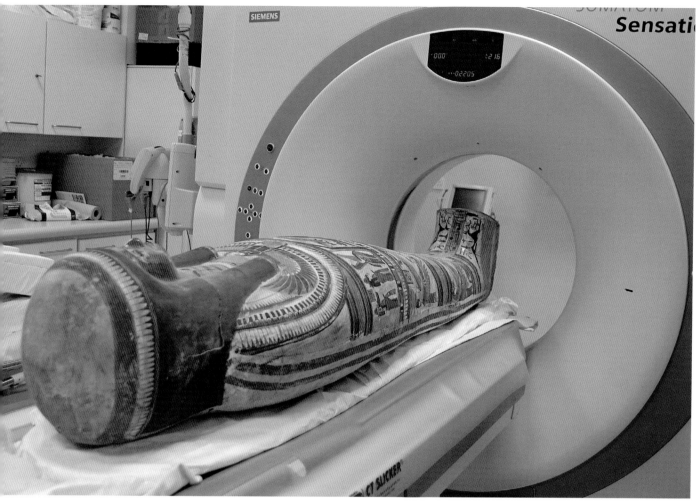

ABOVE The mummy of
Nesperennub entering the
CT scanner at University
College Hospital, London,
December 2007.

RIGHT A frontal topogram or
CT scout image of the contents
of the case is displayed on a
monitor while the scanning
proceeds.

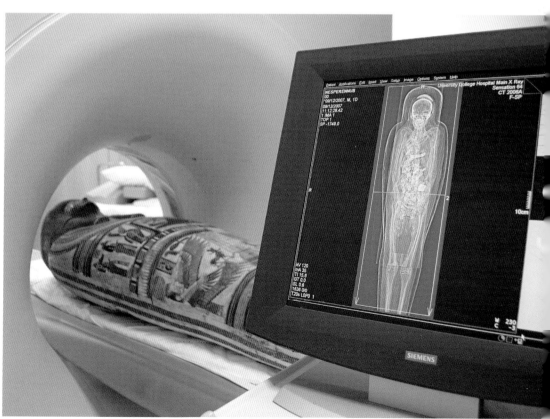

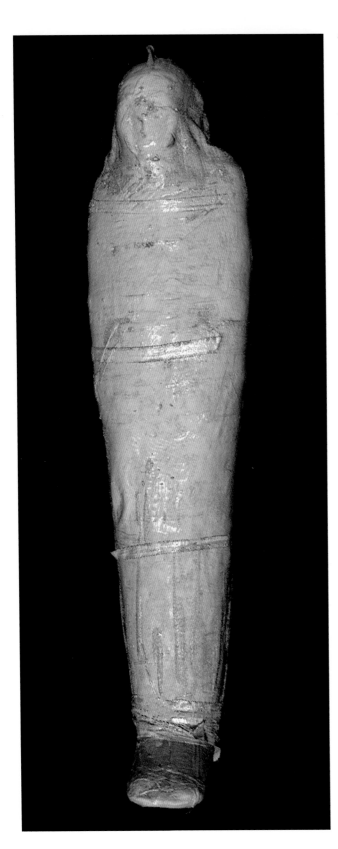

THESE four images demonstrate how the 3D data can be used to perform a 'virtual unwrapping' and autopsy of the mummy of Nesperennub. Any feature inside or outside the body can be revealed and scrutinized in detail.

As the beam of radiation passes through the mummy-case it is attenuated by the various structures and materials it encounters. The degree of attenuation is measured in units on the Hounsfield scale, which is effectively an indication of the relative density of the different contents of the mummy-case. By instructing the computer to display structures of a specific density – such as that of human bone, for example – the investigator can visualize the skeleton or any part of it, such as the skull or pelvis. The forms and developmental state of such features can provide important evidence for assessing sex or age.

While dense materials such as bone are relatively easy to distinguish in CT data, substances of lower densities such as organic soft tissue, textile or resin can pose a greater challenge. The outer surface of the wrapped body can be visualized clearly (left) and the many layers of linen wrappings which lie underneath may be seen in cross-sectional CT slices (pp. 34–5), but it is not so easy to examine them layer-by-layer, because they are all of similar density.

The surviving soft tissue of a mummified body usually has a density very different to that of a living person. Because it is desiccated and may be heavily impregnated with resin it can be difficult to distinguish from denser substances such as bone. However, these soft tissues can nevertheless be visualized.

LEFT The appearance of the outer wrappings; NEAR RIGHT, the surviving soft tissues of the body; CENTRE RIGHT, section through the body showing the interior of the skull and torso; FAR RIGHT, the skeleton together with amulets and objects made from high density materials such as stone and metal.

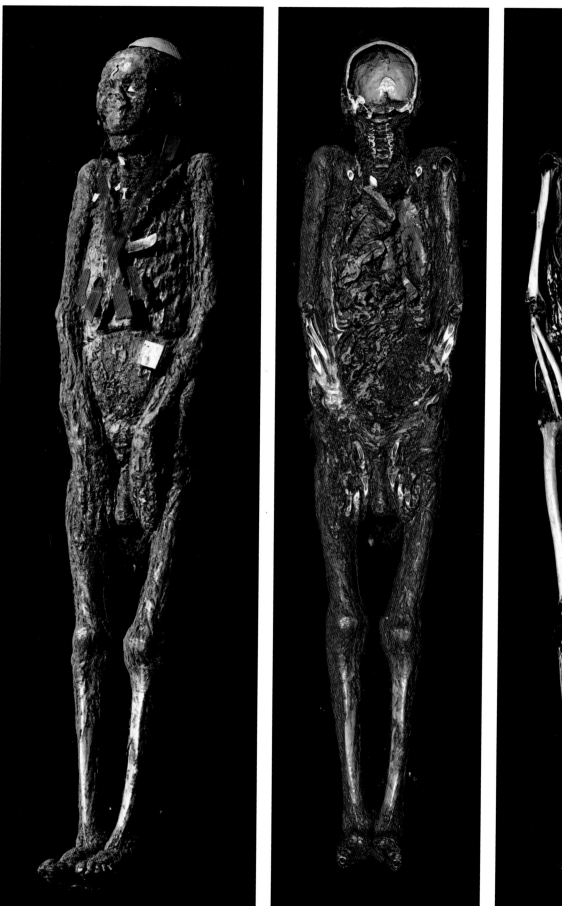
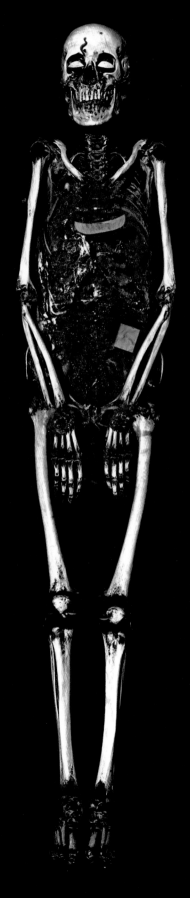

SOFT TISSUE PRESERVATION IN NESPERENNUB

When a body was mummified, the head was treated with special care. It was thought to be important that the dead person should have the use of their eyes, ears, nose and mouth, just as they had done in life (p. 25). Also a life-like rendering of the face was considered an essential element of the transfigured corpse. At some periods a mask was placed over the wrappings of the mummy, showing the deceased in an idealized manner. But at the time of Nesperennub, more attention was paid to mak-

ing the actual face appear lifelike beneath the bandages. This was often done by inserting packing materials such as linen, sand, mud or sawdust under the skin to fill out the shrunken features. There are signs that Nesperennub's body was treated in this way; some areas (particularly the throat) have clearly been stuffed with some unidentifiable material.

It was also common for the body to be painted (red for men, yellow for women) to resemble a statue, and for artificial eyes to be put into the eye sockets. The 3D images show that the soft tissues of Nesperennub's face are well

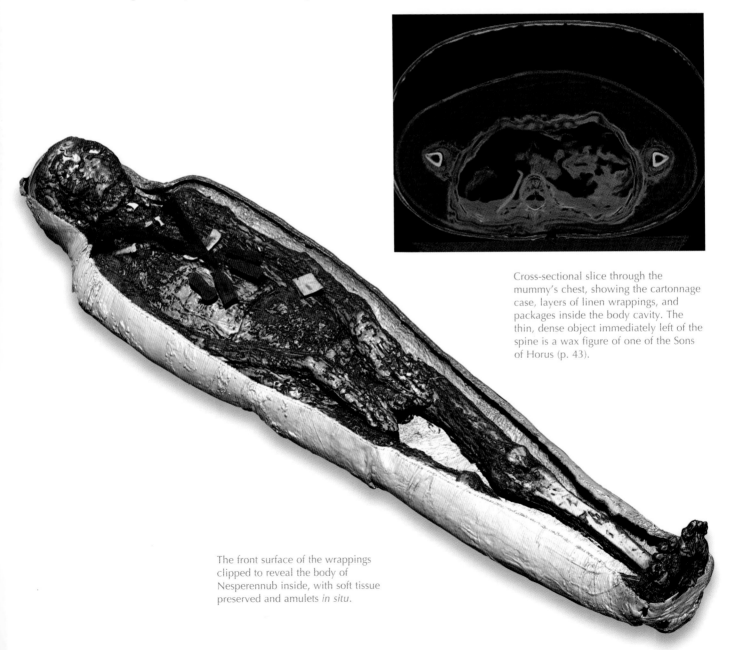

Cross-sectional slice through the mummy's chest, showing the cartonnage case, layers of linen wrappings, and packages inside the body cavity. The thin, dense object immediately left of the spine is a wax figure of one of the Sons of Horus (p. 43).

The front surface of the wrappings clipped to reveal the body of Nesperennub inside, with soft tissue preserved and amulets in situ.

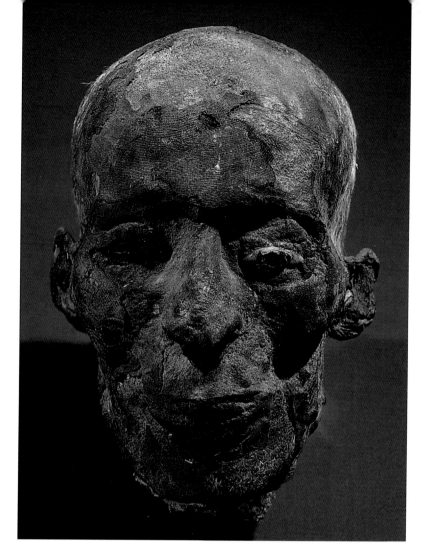

Unwrapped head of an unidentified man with artificial eye remaining in the left socket. Egypt, Third Intermediate Period, c.1070–664 BC. H. 23 cm. British Museum EA 67815.

BELOW Cross-section of the head of Nesperennub's cartonnage case, showing layers of wrappings, the skull and artificial eyes as dense (white) objects in the orbits.

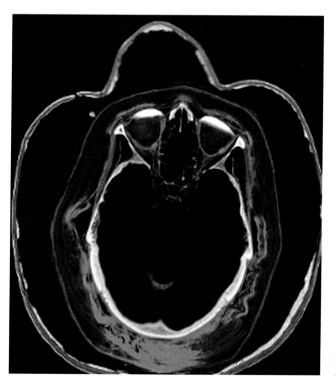

preserved, with the nose, mouth and ears all clearly visible. Artificial eyes are present in the orbits. They are made of a dense material, perhaps stone or opaque glass. No hair can be seen, but this may have been shaved off before death as part of the bodily purification that Nesperennub was obliged to undergo when fulfilling his duties as a priest. Soft tissue is well-preserved throughout the whole body, including the hands, feet, fingers, toes and genitals.

By using clipping planes a section can be taken through the body, revealing bone, soft tissue and objects made of inorganic materials that lie on or under the surface. Such an image (p. 33, centre) shows that the cranium is empty, whereas the chest cavity is filled with bundles of linen, probably soaked in resin. These bundles doubtless contain parts of Nesperennub's internal organs – principally the liver, lungs, stomach and intestines, which were regularly preserved by the embalmers. The packages lie in the right side of the cavity, probably having been inserted by the embalmer through the incision made in the left flank.

AGE AT DEATH AND STATE OF HEALTH

ALTHOUGH the ancient Egyptians were keenly aware of the passage of human life (and regarded 110 years as the ideal age to attain), inscriptions in tombs and on coffins very rarely provide details of the age at which the occupant died. It is the bodies, and above all else, the skeletal remains which offer clues to the age. The development of the teeth and the growth of bones follow a pattern which allows osteologists to estimate the stage of life which an individual had reached, although allowance must be made for regional variations in these growth-rates. Once a person has reached adulthood, the fusing of parts of the skeleton pre-

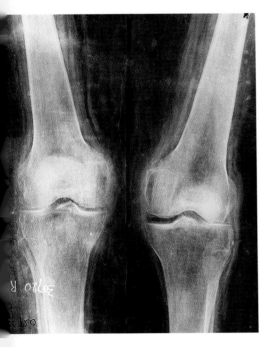

X-ray of the leg-bones. Above and below the knee-joints are faint horizontal lines ('Harris lines') which are indications that Nesperennub underwent periods of arrested growth during his earlier life.

vents further growth; so for older individuals the main clues to age are in the degenerative changes that advancing age brings: wear on or loss of teeth, changes in the bones of the skull, the vertebrae and the ribs, and signs of wear on joints.

The X-rays made in the 1960s, showed that Nesperennub was a full adult. Dawson and Gray estimated his age at thirty to forty years old. This figure was probably deduced from the state of his teeth, which they regarded as moderately worn. The more recent assessment shows that his teeth are well worn, and that he suffered from several dental abscesses (p. 38). The bony plates that form the skull are almost fully joined, an indication that he was a mature adult. Yet the sutures which mark the points at which the plates fuse are still clearly visible and, as these become progressively less obvious with advancing age, it is unlikely that Nesperennub was an elderly man.

The spine, which often shows traces of age-related change and deterioration, appears to be in fairly good condition. There is some osteoarthritis, a build-up of extra bony material at the extremities of the vertebrae. This is a common sign of ageing, yet it is not pronounced in this case. These factors taken together suggest that Nesperennub died when he was middle-aged. We cannot accurately assess how many years he lived, but forty would probably be close to the truth. Life expectancy in ancient Egypt was much lower than it is today. Many infectious diseases and minor injuries, now easily treatable, were fatal then, and the average age at death for men was thirty-five, so Nesperennub would not have considered his lifespan unduly short.

Lines are visible at the ends of the tibiae. These so-called 'Harris lines' are the marks left on the bones by a temporary interruption of the growth process. Periods of illness or nutritional stress are believed to be the cause. The fact that Nesperennub had several of these lines suggests that during his earlier life, when his skeleton was maturing, he either suffered illness or experienced spells of poor diet. Harris lines have been detected in many Egyptian skeletons, even those of persons who were wealthy enough to afford elaborate mummification. It remains uncertain whether these episodes are related to disease or to fluctuations in the food supply from such factors as bad harvests, famine or economic instability.

Once Nesperennub was fully grown and had begun his career as a priest, he would have enjoyed a privileged lifestyle. He would not have had to do hard, manual work – as the absence of broken or fractured bones in his skeleton shows – but would have lived in relative comfort. His diet would have been a healthy and well-balanced one – mainly bread, fruit and vegetables, with beer or wine to drink. He would also have had more meat to eat than the average peasant. Beef and poultry were among the regular offerings made in the temples, and once the god had been satisfied his priests were allowed to dine on what remained.

TOP All Nesperennub's teeth had erupted, with the exception of his third molars (wisdom teeth). This supports the notion that he died before reaching old age.

BOTTOM View of the back of the skull. The bony plates have united but the sutures are still visible, suggesting that Nesperennub was a mature, but not elderly man at the time of his death.

TEETH

The ancient Egyptians suffered from many dental problems. The contamination of their food by windblown sand caused extensive wear on the biting surfaces of the teeth, leading to infections and abscesses. Dental surgery was not practiced – only pharmaceutical remedies being available – and unrelieved toothache must have been widespread.

All of Nesperennub's teeth appear to be present except for the third molars (wisdom teeth) – but often these do not erupt at all. There is quite heavy wear on the biting surfaces of the teeth. This probably exposed the roots in some places and allowed infection to enter, as several abscesses can be seen at the base of the teeth. There is at one particularly noticeable spot on Nesperennub's lower jaw where this seems to have happened; a cavity is apparent at the root of the first molar on the right-hand side. This might be explained as an example of resorption (the retraction of the bony setting of the tooth), but in view of the heavy wear already mentioned it is more likely to be a dental abscess. It would certainly have caused Nesperennub much pain and discomfort, and probably made him irritable and short-tempered.

Images of Nesperennub's teeth. The three-quarter view (right) shows a substantial cavity at the root of the first molar in the lower jaw, probably as a result of an abcess.

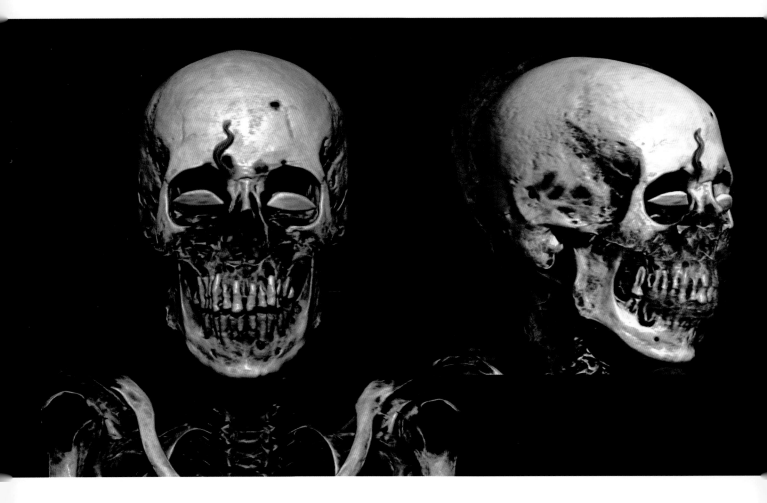

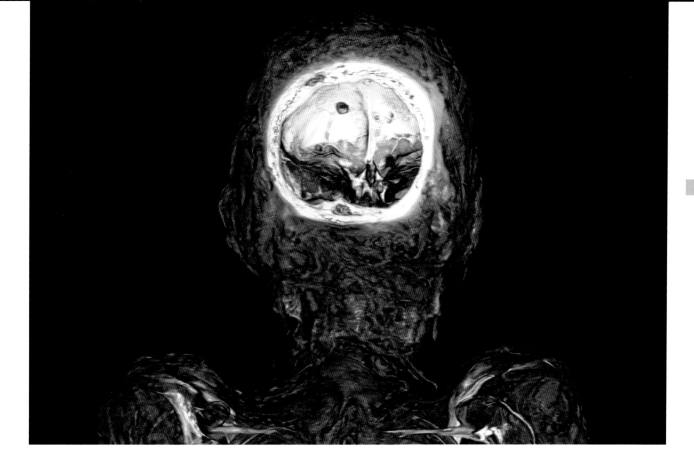

AN ANOMALY IN THE SKULL

Nesperennub's skeleton is complete, with no broken bones or signs of major trauma. However, there is one curious anomaly on his skull. The 3D images show a small cavity or hole in the bone, above the left eye. This hole is not easy to explain. It does not have any connection with the process of mummification; the brain was usually extracted via the nose, and there is no reason to doubt that this was done in the case of Nesperennub. There are no traces of cracking or splitting of the bone, as might be expected if the hole had been caused by a blow or a wound with a sharp instrument or weapon.

A third possibility is that Nesperennub had suffered from an illness which attacked the bone of his skull. The axial CT images show that the abnormal cavity mainly affected the interior of the skull, and that the bone was not completely pierced. This would suggest that the damage came from inside. If it is not a healed injury, then some form of tumour might have been responsible. After the brain had been removed during mummification, the only trace of the condition remaining would be this mark on the bone.

However, perhaps a more plausible explanation is that the cavity was caused by an anomaly of the vascular system. It is noticeable that one of the traces left behind on the frontal bone by the blood vessels of the brain passes through this spot. A knot of blood vessels here could have eroded the bony surface of the skull, creating a small hol-

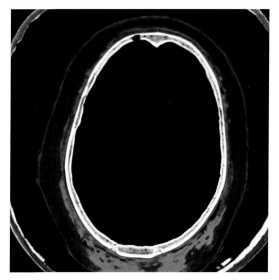

TOP View into the skull through a clipping plane, showing the abnormal cavity above the left eye-socket.

ABOVE CT image of the skull showing the cavity above the eye. This view shows that it had almost pierced the frontal bone of the skull.

low depression called a *nidus* ('nest'). It might be possible for a patient to live with this condition without difficulty, but if the vessel were to rupture it might result in death. Such an event could have ended Nesperennub's life but it is impossible to prove that this happened.

MUMMIFICATION:
removing the internal organs

THE first task which the embalmer performed was the extraction of the brain. The Greek historian Herodotus recorded that, in his day (c.450 BC), this was done via the nose, and examination of many mummies has confirmed this. A small chisel was used to perforate the small bones at the top of the nose, and a metal rod was inserted into the skull cavity. Using this, the brain, which would have partly liquefied already in the hot climate, was drawn in pieces down the nostril and disposed of. The scans of Nesperennub confirm that this method was followed during his mummification. The ethmoid bone at the top of the nose was broken away to gain access to the skull cavity, but the operation was carefully done as the nasal plate is visible still *in situ*. The brain itself was removed completely, but the 3D images show traces of a thin, papery substance clinging to the inside of the skull at the back of the head – these are almost certainly the remains of the meninges (or membranes that surround the brain), left behind after the process of removal.

Also visible on the bony surface of the interior of the skull is the imprint left behind by the blood vessels of the brain.

LEFT A clipping plane through the centre of the skull, revealing the empty brain-case, and the traces of membrane at the lower left side.

BELOW CT image of the skull, showing intentional damage made to the nasal bones in order to extract the brain during mummification.

RIGHT 'Virtual probe' entering skull via the passage left by the operation performed by the embalmers.

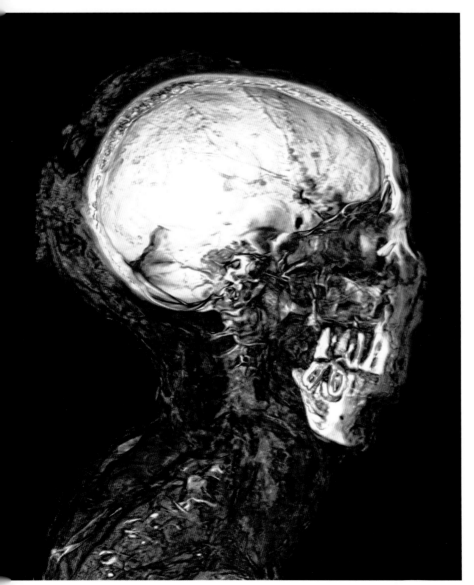

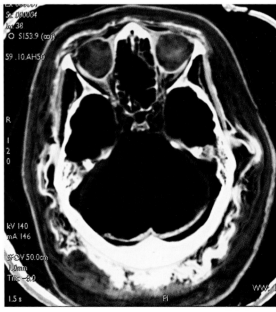

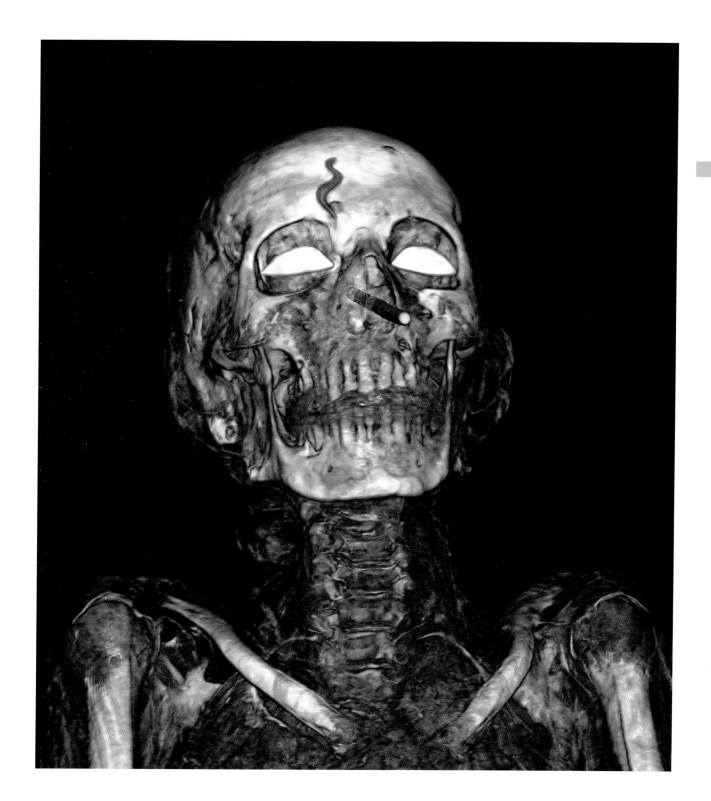

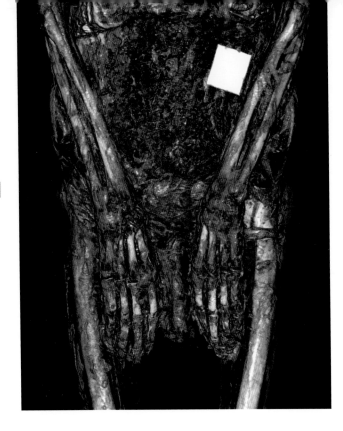

ABOVE Metal incision plate from a mummy. It bears the *wedjat*, or Eye of Horus, a common protective device which symbolically 'healed' the embalming incision. Egypt, Third Intermediate Period, c.1069–664 BC. H. 8 cm. British Museum EA 8409.

LEFT Front view of the lower abdomen showing bones and other dense material. The rectangular object lying over the left flank is a metal plate covering the incision made to extract the internal organs.

BOTTOM Set of four calcite canopic jars inscribed for Gemenefhorbak. Egypt, 26th Dynasty, c.664–525 BC. H. 42–46 cm. British Museum EA 36637, 36638, 36639, 36640.

Next, the embalmer made an incision on the left side of the abdomen. Through this almost all of the internal organs were removed. The corpse was then covered with natron, a natural compound of salts, which – over a period of about forty days – absorbed all the bodily fluids. At the end of this process the body was thoroughly desiccated and there was no means for destructive bacteria to thrive.

The heart was usually given special treatment. The organ was regarded as the centre of the person's being, both physically and spiritually, and as the location of the mind and memory. It was necessary to survival after death, and it would be weighed in the balance to enable the gods to assess its owner's character (p. 27). For these reasons the heart was left in place when all the other contents of the chest were removed. However, in the mummy of Nesperennub the heart is difficult to identify – perhaps it was not successfully preserved?

Some of the internal organs (usually the liver, lungs, stomach and intestines) were also preserved and wrapped in resin-soaked bandages. For many centuries these bundles were placed in four vessels now called canopic jars, and stored in the tomb in a special niche or close to the coffin. From c.1100 BC to c.700 BC (and often in later centuries) they were simply replaced in the body cavity, each

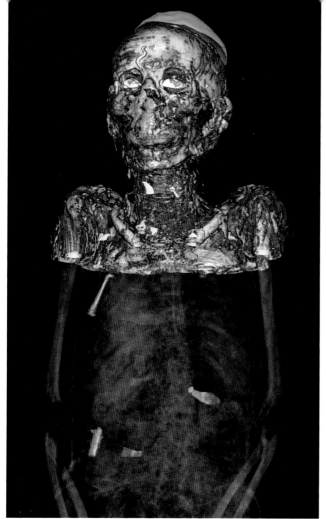
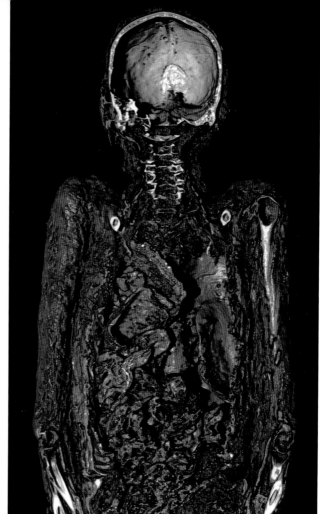

package accompanied by a wax figurine representing one of four protective deities, the Sons of Horus. The 3D images of Nesperennub's chest show clearly that four bundles lie inside, and that each of these is accompanied by a figure of one of the Sons of Horus.

In Nesperennub's time it was usual for the embalmers to insert packing materials beneath the skin in an attempt to restore a lifelike appearance to the shriveled face and limbs. The substances used included resin, sand and linen, and they were introduced sometimes through incisions in the skin or through the body's natural orifices such as the mouth. There are signs that some of these manipulations were carried out on Nesperennub; the trachea and tongue seem to have been removed and resin has been detected inside the mouth and neck. It was also smeared over the mouth, and the exterior of the head seems to have been liberally coated with this substance (see below, p. 50–1).

TOP LEFT View of the interior of Nesperennub's chest cavity, showing three of the four wax figures of the Sons of Horus. These are probably associated with the packages containing internal organs, visible on the right of the image.

TOP RIGHT A clipping plane through the front of Nesperennub's mummy revealing the packages containing the internal organs on the right of the chest cavity.

LEFT Four figurines of resin representing the Sons of Horus. Such images were placed inside the chest of the mummy to give magical protection to the internal organs. Third Intermediate Period, c.1069–664 BC. H. 14–17 cm.
British Museum EA 15562, 15571, 15579, 15580.

MUMMIFICATION:
amulets and other trappings

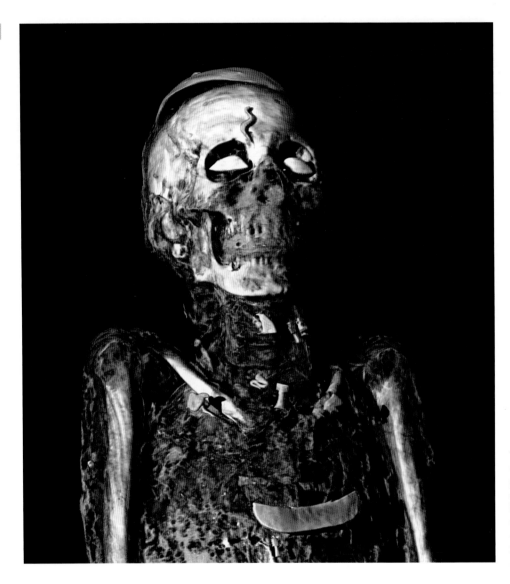

This image highlights objects of various different materials, placed on or near to the surface of the body: a clay bowl at the back of the skull (pp.50–1), a snake amulet on the forehead, artificial eyes in the orbits, and groups of amulets and a winged pectoral ornament on the chest.

AFTER the preservation of the corpse came the lengthy process of adorning and wrapping it. This often involved placing items of jewellery, amulets and other trappings on the body and between the layers of bandages.

An important way of giving a person special powers or protection was through the use of amulets. These small images or figurines were usually made of stone, metal or glazed ceramic, and their power was supposed to reside in their shape, their colour, the material they were made from, and any magical texts inscribed on them or spoken over them. Amulets were worn by the living and were often placed on the bodies of the dead,

within the wrappings. The mummy of Tutankhamun had a profusion of amulets, and several are visible within the bandages of Nesperennub. The position of the amulets was also important; many were placed on the neck and upper body, regarded by the Egyptians as the most vulnerable areas.

One of the most intriguing features revealed by the 3D images of Nesperennub is a small object in the shape of a snake, which lies just above his right eye. It takes the form of the cobra, the hieroglyphic sign for the sound 'dj'. The snake is not simply a flat silhouette, but when viewed from an angle is seen to be a 3D object. However, it does not show up on conventional X-rays and seems to

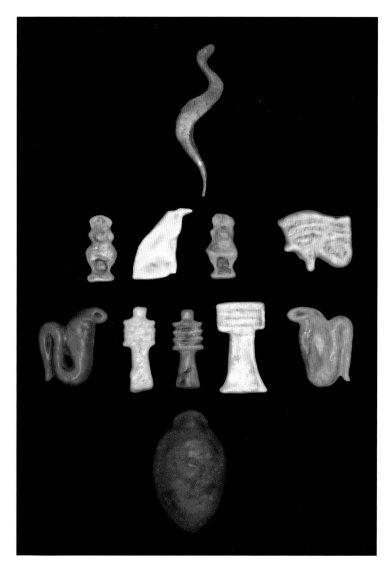

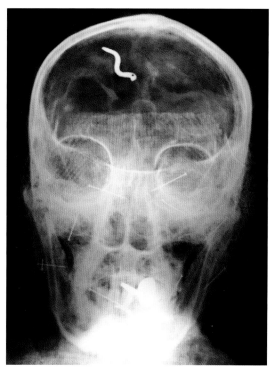

ABOVE X-ray of the skull of a Late Period mummy showing a snake amulet of thin metal, apparently attached to the inner wrappings above the right eye. Rijksmuseum van Oudheden, Leiden.

LEFT Images of the main amulets, isolated and artificially coloured to represent the materials of which they are conjectured to have been made. From top: snake amulet, perhaps of wax; baboons, vulture and *wedjat* eye, probably faience (non-clay based ceramic); serpents and *djed* pillars, probably faience; a heart amulet, perhaps of stone.

be made of a substance of relatively low density; wax is a possibility, since this was believed by the Egyptians to have magical properties and was used to fashion objects and figurines that were placed on mummies. The object is in very close proximity to the face of Nesperennub, and if not actually in contact with his skin it must be attached to the innermost layer of wrappings.

An amulet in the form of a snake's head was a fairly common element of the trappings of mummies after the New Kingdom. They are associated with the protection of the throat and their main purpose was probably to ward off snake bites. However, these examples are usually made of a red-coloured material such as jasper.

Snake amulets that represent the complete animal are unusual. One made of gold was found at the neck of Tutankhamun, another, of thin gold, was found on the head of the mummy of a priest from Thebes who died *c.*935 BC, and a third has been detected by X-rays over the right eye of a Late Period mummy in the Rijksmuseum van Oudheden in Leiden. Because these snake-amulets are so rare, their precise significance is unknown. The positioning of some of them on the forehead might possibly suggest some connection with the *uraeus* serpent. This protective cobra goddess regularly adorned the headdress of the pharaoh, but occasionally appeared on mummies and masks of private individuals.

Nesperennub's snake, then, may have had two magical functions – to guard him against evil forces in the afterlife and to suggest that he had gained a higher status in the world of the gods – more akin to that of a king.

A group of four small amulets can be seen clustered at Nesperennub's throat. They are very clearly recognizable by their shapes. One is the *djed* pillar, a symbol of the god Osiris, ruler of the realm of the dead. According to spell 155 in the 'Book of the Dead', a *djed* pillar of gold should be placed at the throat of the deceased. When the proper words were recited the amulet would become effective and would guarantee access to the divine realm and the entourage of Osiris. In a more general sense it would confer stability and the power to stand up, resurrected.

With the *djed* pillar is a vulture facing to the left. This amulet probably represents the protective goddess Nekhbet. The group is completed by two identical amulets in the form of a baboon squatting on his haunches and wearing on his head the disc of the moon. The god Thoth is often represented in this form. He played an important role in helping the dead to attain eternal life, not least at the weighing of the heart, the critical judgement which determined who deserved to enter the eternal realm and who did not. Alternatively these figurines might be depictions of Khons, who could assume the same form; since Nesperennub was a priest of this god it is possible that the amulets were intended as images of the deity whom he served in life.

These four amulets were probably threaded on to a cord wound around the neck. Similar groups have been found on several mummies of Theban priests from the Twenty-first Dynasty, and this custom was still maintained during Nesperennub's time. In the centuries that followed his death the number of amulets placed on the neck and other parts of the body increased.

At the base of the neck, lying a little above the right clavicle, is an amulet of roughly oval shape with a small projection at the upper end. Its shape and position strongly suggest that it is a heart-amulet. Spell 30 of the 'Book of the Dead' related to the function of these amulets. They are sometimes inscribed with the words of the spell on the base in hieroglyphs. This commanded the dead man's heart not to reveal any potentially damning information about him when he came into the presence of the gods. It was feared that this might happen during the judgement, which every mortal had to undergo, when the heart was weighed in a balance against an image of right and justice (pp. 26–7). In Nesperennub's time this spell was more commonly written on a large amulet carved from dark green or black stone, representing the scarab beetle – a manifestation of the sun god and a symbol of the renewal of life. However, there is no trace of a heart scarab within Nesperennub's wrappings – perhaps the heart amulet alone was intended to fulfil this function.

A little further down the chest, in the middle, a *uraeus* serpent and another *djed* pillar can be seen. The CT scans show that these objects lie at a higher level than the heart

Winged solar disc painted on the lid of a wooden coffin. Thebes, 22nd Dynasty, c.800 BC. L. 167 cm. British Museum EA 29578.

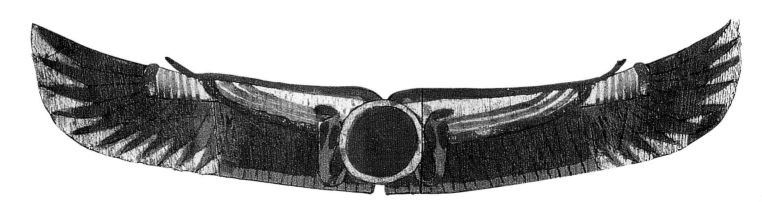

TOP Faience (non-clay based ceramic) amulets of types visible on the mummy of Nesperennub: (LEFT) *djed* pillar, H. 11 cm; (CENTRE) *wedjat* eye, W. 5 cm; (RIGHT) rearing cobra, H. 4 cm. Third Intermediate or Late Period, c.1069–305 BC. British Museum EA 12235, 7321, 12034.

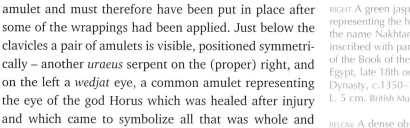

amulet and must therefore have been put in place after some of the wrappings had been applied. Just below the clavicles a pair of amulets is visible, positioned symmetrically – another *uraeus* serpent on the (proper) right, and on the left a *wedjat* eye, a common amulet representing the eye of the god Horus which was healed after injury and which came to symbolize all that was whole and undamaged.

Lower still on the breast lies a pectoral, probably of sheet metal, in the form of outspread wings. Winged figures were commonly painted on coffins at this period (pp. 8, 9, 20) and pectoral ornaments in similar forms are often seen under the wrappings of mummies. The outline of this example (without trace of a head or the legs of a bird) suggests that it represents a winged solar disc, rather than a falcon, vulture or scarab beetle (the most plausible alternatives). Just below it lies another *djed* pillar.

In addition to the amulets on the trunk, there are four clusters of small objects, one on each hand and one on each arm. All of them are rather difficult to identify, as their shapes are not very distinctive. Other mummies of the Twenty-first Dynasty have been found with amulets tied around the arm with cords; these are sometimes beads, but on several mummies of priests of Amun from this period there is a pairing of a *djed* pillar on one arm and a plaque bearing a figure of Thoth on the other. Those on Nesperennub's arms seem to be beads or small pierced pendants of indeterminate form. On each hand

RIGHT A green jasper amulet representing the heart. It bears the name Nakhtamun and is inscribed with part of spell 30B of the Book of the Dead. Egypt, late 18th or early 19th Dynasty, c.1350–1250 BC. L. 5 cm. British Museum EA 15619.

BELOW A dense object lying above the spine of Nesperennub. Its shape and position suggest that it is a heart amulet, and its relatively high density may indicate that it is made of stone.

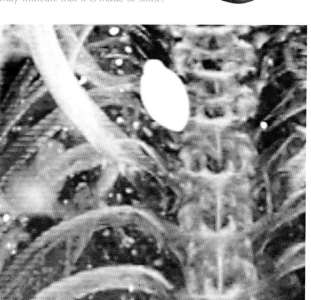

a group of small objects can be seen: on the left hand a cylindrical bead, a small *wedjat* eye and two unidentified items seem to be attached to one finger; on the right hand is another tubular bead and *wedjat*, with a snake and a *wadj* amulet.

Just beneath Nesperennub's outer wrappings, narrow bands of a relatively low density material can be seen passing over the shoulders and crossing on the chest. At the lower ends are tabs of a trapezoidal shape. These objects, known to Egyptologists as stolae or 'mummy-braces', are usually made of leather, dyed red, with terminals of undyed leather with red edging. Gods such as Osiris are often depicted wearing them, and from about 1100 BC they began to be included among the trappings of mummies, perhaps to promote the idea that through the rituals of mummification the dead were el-

ABOVE Terminal tab of a leather stole from a mummy. It is embossed with an image of King Osorkon I before the goddess Amunet. Thebes, 22nd Dynasty, c 924–889 BC. British Museum EA 66642 (Donated by R. M. Bridge).

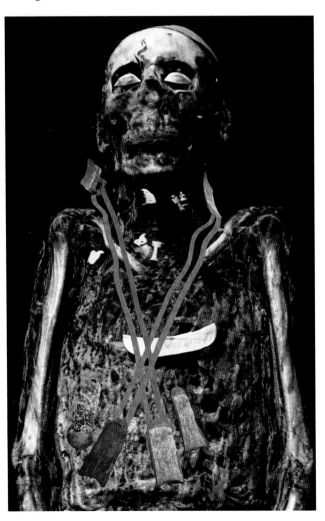

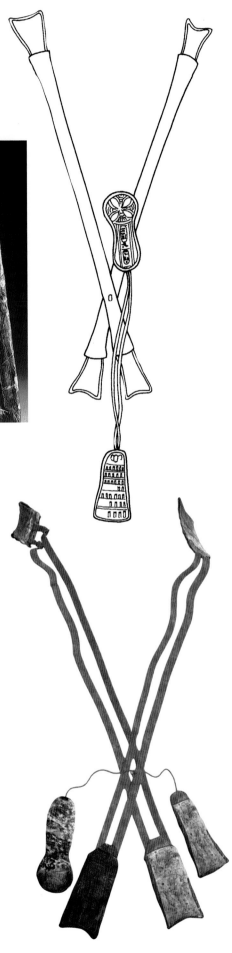

ABOVE RIGHT Drawing of a pair of leather stoles with amulets threaded on thongs, from a Theban mummy of the 22nd Dynasty.

BELOW RIGHT Artificially coloured image of the stoles and pendants from the mummy Nesperennub.

LEFT Mummy of Nesperennub showing leather stoles and pendants *in situ* on the chest.

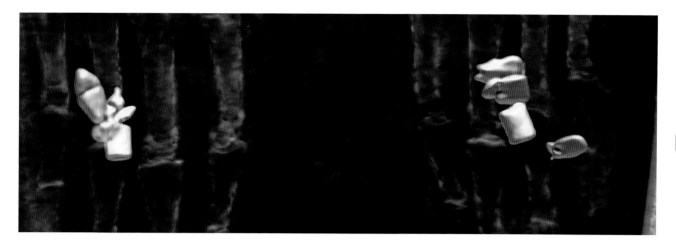

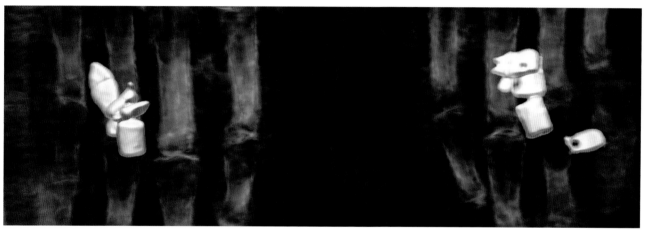

evated to a status similar to that of gods. The braces are common on mummies of the Twenty-first and Twenty-second Dynasties, and are often painted on the coffins and cartonnage cases of this period; they are shown, for example, on the coffin of Ankhefenkhons (p. 9).

Images of the front and rear surfaces of both hands, showing beads and small amules threaded on strings around the fingers.

The upper ends of Nesperennub's stolae also have tabs, and these are not positioned on his back but lie on his shoulders. He was also equipped with two other leather pendants of different forms – one resembles a necklace counterpoise, the other a *menit*. These can be seen clearly lying on the chest close to the brace-tabs and attached at the crossing point of the braces by means of a very thin cord or thong, again probably of leather. Similar examples have been found on mummies unwrapped in the nineteenth century. Stola-tabs and pendants are of value to historians. They often bear embossed inscriptions that name the king who reigned at the time of the mummy's burial. The 3D images do not tell us whether the tabs on Nesperennub's mummy are inscribed. If they are, and with the development of more sensitive scanning technology, it may be possible one day to read the inscriptions and fix the date of his death precisely.

THE MYSTERIOUS BOWL:
an embalmer's mistake?

THE cloudy X-ray images obtained in the 1960s had shown that an opaque object lay on the top of Nesperennub's head, underneath the linen wrappings. Gray and Dawson, who drew up the report on the X-rays, thought that this might be a human placenta or afterbirth, which the Egyptians revered as though it were a twin or double of the individual; they claimed to have found a dried placenta on the heads of two other mummies dating to around 1000 BC. However, the new 3D images of Nesperennub immediately revealed that the object on the head was not a placenta, but a shallow bowl of coarse, unfired clay.

The shape of the bowl and the nature of its fabric have been revealed with astonishing clarity. Its irregular form indicates that it was shaped by hand, not on a potter's wheel. There are even impressions in the surface which correspond to the marks of fingers and a thumb.

A clay bowl is a most unusual object to find within the wrappings of a mummy. It does not belong to any known ritual aspect of embalming. The bone of the skull underneath it is not damaged in any way, nor does the bowl seem to be fulfilling any practical purpose. Its crude make points instead to it having been part of the embalmers' working equipment – but why should it have been placed within the wrappings?

When the mummy's head is viewed in 3D from different angles, and under a variety of visualization settings, an important clue to the bowl's function becomes apparent. Adhering to the top and back of Nesperennub's head, and also to the bowl itself, is what appears to be a thick deposit of some glutinous matter. Its density and its appearance suggest that it is a thick, semi-liquid substance which has solidified. It is probably resin, which was used extensively in mummification. The resin, collected from trees or plants, would be heated until molten and then smeared or brushed over the skin. The clay bowl may have been used by the embalmers to hold some of this resin. Large quantities seem to have been poured over Nesperennub while he lay on the embalming bed, and much of it ran down and began to solidify at the back of his head. Perhaps the embalmers placed the bowl on the head to collect some of this surplus liquid. An experiment using a facsimile of the bowl has shown that it could easily have rested at the back of the head while the body lay supine.

What happened then we do not know. Perhaps the resin hardened unexpectedly quickly, cementing the bowl firmly to the skull. Discovering their mistake, the embalmers would surely have tried to remove the bowl. An area on the back of the head from which the skin appears to have been torn away may represent an unsuccessful attempt to prise off the lumps of resin that anchored the bowl in place. Realising that the bowl could not be removed without causing further damage, the embalmers may have decided to proceed with the wrapping of the

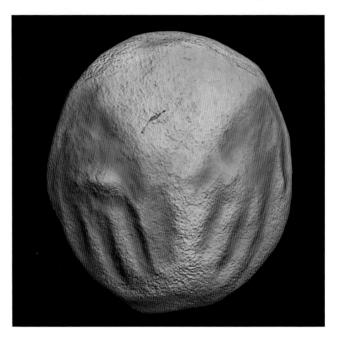

Digital replica of the clay dowl. The impressions visible on the surface were probably made by the hands of the person who shaped the vessel.

body, hoping that their mistake would pass unnoticed. It would not be the first or the last time that Egyptian embalmers made errors. Investigations of other mummies have revealed that parts of the body were sometimes lost or displaced, that small tools and probes were left behind inside the corpse (the nightmare of the modern surgeon), and that insects and even small rodents obtained free access to the dead. Since Nesperennub's relatives would not have been present during his mummification, this particular piece of professional negligence would remain a secret for 2,800 years.

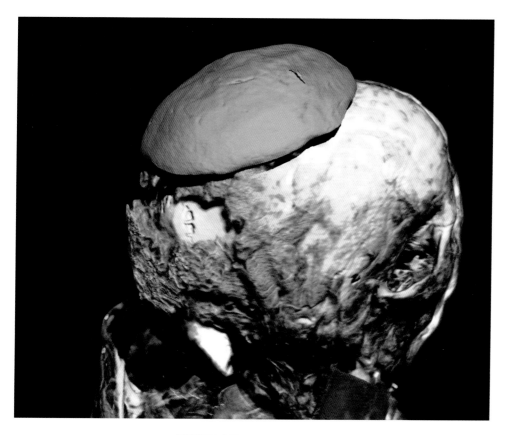

Two views of the bowl *in situ* at the rear of the mummy's head.

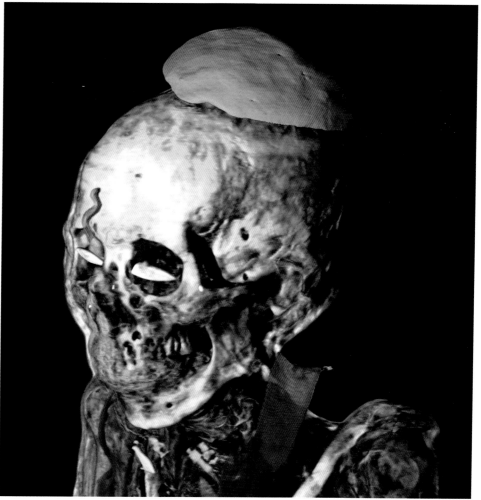

WRAPPING THE BODY

WRAPPING the body was a very important part of the mummification process. Not only did it ensure that all the essential parts of the corpse remained together, it also helped to create the correct appearance for the dead person. The distinctive mummy shape and the outer trappings emphasized the idea that the deceased had been transformed into an eternal being, one who possessed the attributes of powerful gods. The wrappings of the mummy were even supposed to be made by the gods themselves. Inscriptions refer to the dead person receiving wrappings from Tayet, goddess of weaving, or from the weavers of the goddess Neith.

Linen, made from the flax plant, was the commonest textile used by the ancient Egyptians. Clothes and bed-covers were usually woven from linen, and these items were often recycled as mummy wrappings. Both complete sheets and long strips like bandages were used for wrapping the dead. The amount of linen used varied; one mummy was wrapped in over 375 square metres of cloth.

CT scans of Nesperennub clearly show the many layers of wrappings put on by the embalmers. Those closest to the body would be soaked in molten resin to help them to stick to the skin. The usual procedure was for the head, arms and legs to be individually wrapped first. After this, large sheets would alternate with more layers of bandages. The final layer was a single sheet or shroud, covering the whole body. This would often be dyed a reddish pink colour – perhaps to suggest that the dead person was reborn through the life-giving power of the sun god.

In the most elaborate embalming, putting on the wrappings was done with great ceremony. An Egyptian text known as the 'Ritual of Embalming' records the key steps and explains that each piece of cloth had special religious significance. Besides the bandages, amulets were placed between the layers of cloth, and at some periods a papyrus roll containing religious texts was inserted among the wrappings.

The 3D images of Nesperennub clearly show the outer shroud which envelops his mummy from head to foot, the edges neatly folded over beneath the feet. Four strips of bandage can also be seen, tied laterally around the body to hold the shroud in place. They are carefully positioned at traditional locations – the upper breast, abdomen, knees and ankles. There are also signs that two further strips were positioned diagonally over the shoulders, crossing on the chest.

Examples of linen mummy wrappings.
Egypt, 25th–26th Dynasty (747–525 BC).
L. 90 cm; 526 cm; 256 cm.
British Museum EA 6516, 6518, 6542.

The shroud covering the inner wrappings, secured in place by four lateral strips of cloth (RIGHT). The shroud was folded beneath the feet to ensure that no creases were visible on the frontal surface (BELOW).

CONSTRUCTING THE CARTONNAGE CASE

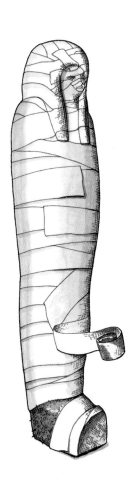

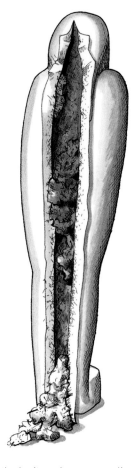

Construction of a cartonnage mummy-case:
1 A mummy-shaped core is constructed from mud mixed with straw, perhaps built around a lightweight frame of reeds.

2 Up to twenty layers of linen soaked in glue or plaster are applied to the core, closely following its shape.

3 While the linen layers are still pliable, the core material is extracted in pieces through an opening in the back.

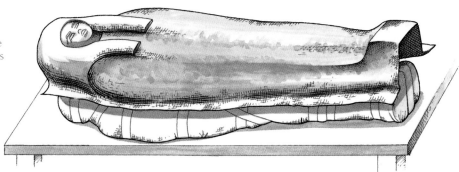

4 The hollow cartonnage shell, still flexible, is fitted around the wrapped mummy, and the rear flaps drawn together.

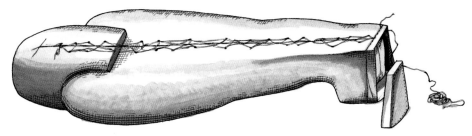

5 Cord is threaded through holes punched along the rear edges, and the mummy is secured inside. The open foot-end of the case is sealed with a wooden board, attached with pegs or cord.

ONCE wrapping had been completed, the mummy was put into a coffin – often, indeed, into two, three or even four coffins – one inside the other. Egyptian coffins were usually made of wood or stone, and were either rectangular or carved to imitate the shape of the mummy. The majority consisted of two parts – a lid and a case to hold the body. But in the ninth and eighth centuries BC, when Nesperennub lived, inner coffins were often made of cartonnage, a laminate of linen and plaster. Layers of cloth were carefully built up around a disposable core, probably of mud and straw, which reproduced the shape of the mummy. When complete, the core was removed, leaving a tough shell of linen. The mummy was put inside this through an opening at the back, and the two flaps were drawn together and tightly laced with string, like a shoe.

A coating of fine white plaster was applied to the outer surface, and inscriptions and religious images painted on. The advantages of this type of coffin were that it was cheaper and easier to make than one of stone or wood, and that once the mummy was sealed inside, it could not be removed again without damaging the painted case. This was a precaution against thieves, who sometimes stole coffins and sold them to new purchasers after erasing the name of the original owner.

This unscrupulous practice was widespread among cemetery employees at Thebes *c.*1000–900 BC, and might have contributed to the growing popularity of cartonnage cases. They ensured that the dead person inside the case would not be deprived of the all-important religious imagery painted on the surface, and they also preserved the name – regarded by the Egyptians as a key element of the human being, which must survive if he/she was to enter the afterlife.

6 When the cartonnage has dried and hardened, painted decoration is applied to the exterior over a ground of fine white plaster.

COFFINS: decoration

BESIDES providing physical protection for the corpse, Egyptian coffins were supposed to equip the occupant with magical attributes and ritual knowledge to assist him/her on the passage into the afterlife. This role was expressed through the shape and colouring of the coffins, and through the texts and images on their surfaces. At some periods of Egyptian history the most important of these details were put on the walls of the tomb chapel or on papyrus rolls buried with the mummy. But at the time in which Nesperennub lived very few decorated tombs were being made for private individuals, and funerary papyri were no longer in use, so the surfaces of the coffins became the main vehicle for displaying religious images and writings. Because of the limited space available, images were carefully designed to convey different levels of meaning simultaneously.

The 'anthropoid', or mummiform, shape of the coffin reflected the divine status which the dead attained. Nesperennub's outer wooden coffin is simple in design, with a painted face, wig and collar and a line of inscription identifying the occupant. The reddish colouring of the background associates the deceased with the sun god.

The coffin was also regarded symbolically as a kind of cocoon. Inside, the dead person lay like a child in its mother's womb, ready to be reborn into the afterlife. Figures of important goddesses, such as Nut or Hathor, were often painted on the inside of the coffin. These images often have their arms outstretched to enfold the mummy in a protective embrace, emphasizing the maternal aspect.

The main concentration of religious images was usually put on to the inner coffin, in close proximity to the mummy, and this applies to the cartonnage case of Nesperennub. He is surrounded by figures of gods and religious symbols, carefully arranged according to an underlying plan which would help to bring about Nesperennub's rebirth and eternal life.

On the breast is a scarab with the head and wings of a falcon. The scarab beetle, Khepri represented the sun at dawn, while the falcon was more closely associated with the daytime sun. Beneath are two pairs of gods in mummy-shape representing the Sons of Horus, whose names were Imsety, Hapy, Duamutef and Qebhsennuef. They protected the internal organs of the mummy, but they were also believed to help raise the sun god into the sky each

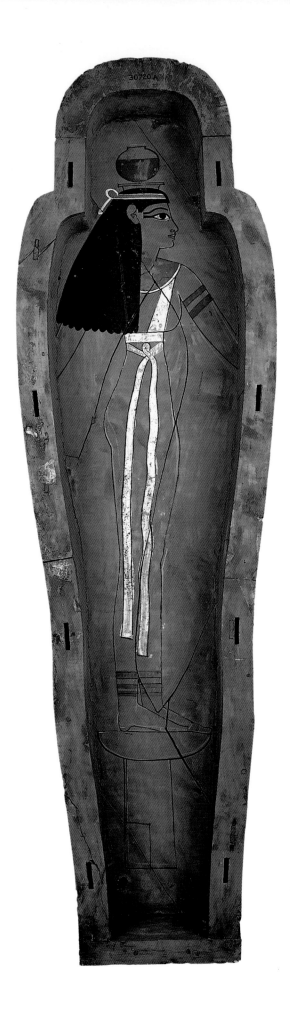

The upper section of the cartonnage case (p. 8), on which
is depicted the sun god as a scarab beetle with a falcon's
head and wings. Below, two serpent goddesses and the
four Sons of Horus flank a mummified falcon representing
the funerary god Sokar-Osiris.
British Museum EA 30720.

OPPOSITE Interior of Nesperennub's wooden coffin (p. 4).
On the floor is painted the figure of a goddess, whose
arms extend on to the side walls in a symbolic gesture of
protection. The jar-hieroglyph above her head indicates
that she is Nut, the sky goddess and mother of Osiris,
although her feet rest on a hieroglyphic group signifying
the name of the goddess Nephthys.
British Museum EA 30720.

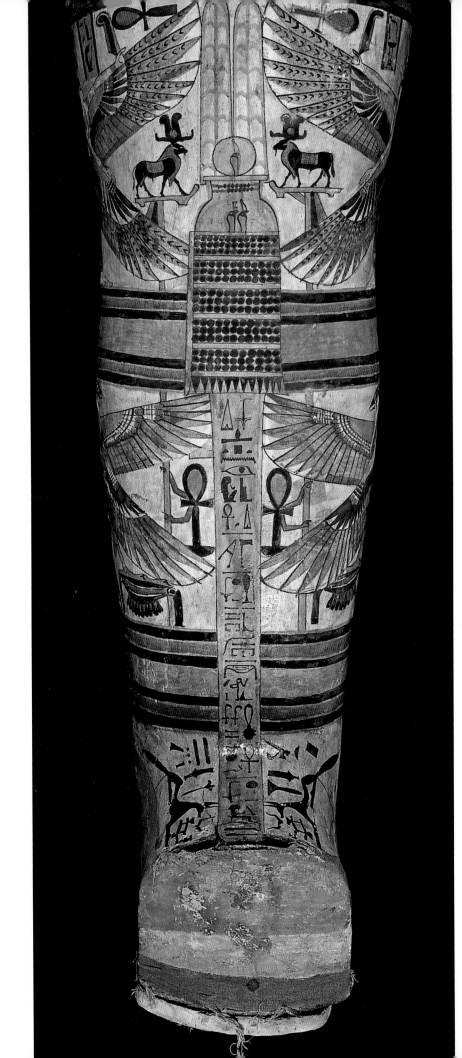

The lower section of the cartonnage case is dominated by the domed and feathered fetish of Abydos, emblem of the god Osiris, which is flanked by ram-standards, winged goddesses and falcons. British Museum EA 30720.

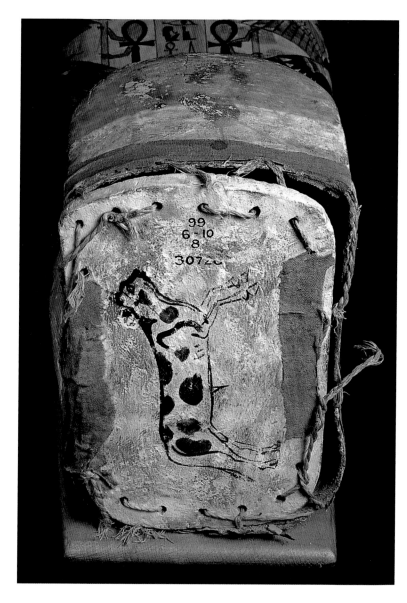

On the footboard of the cartonnage case is an image of the Apis bull, a manifestation of the god Ptah of Memphis. One of his functions was to carry the dead to their tombs, and on later coffins this motif includes an image of the mummy borne on the bull's back. British Museum EA 30720.

and images of deities. Two of these, bearing ram-figures, are shown on the mummy-case of Nesperennub. Each standard is supported by an *ankh*, the sign of life, which is provided with human arms. Through the painting of the fetish on the mummy-case, the dead person was closely identified with Osiris. Just as the god was believed to have risen from the dead, so Nesperennub would be restored to life for eternity.

At each side of the Osiris emblem stand the goddesses Isis and Nephthys. They were the sisters of the murdered Osiris who, according to mythology, restored him to life by beating the air with their wings. Here their winged arms convey life and at the same time shield the god's emblem from harm. Below, further protection is provided by two falcons. Although not named here, they are identified on similar mummy-cases as the goddesses Neith and Selkis. At the lower extremity of the case are two jackals representing the god Wepwawet, whose name means the 'Opener of the Ways.' His role was to protect the dead and to guide their footsteps on their passage to the next world – a duty which is reflected in the positioning of these figures at the feet.

The two most important elements of this design are the winged sun god and the emblem of Osiris. Each of these deities was believed to have the power to renew life, and each ruled over a different part of the universe: the sun god's realm was in the sky, and that of Osiris beneath the earth. Every night the two were momentarily joined and rejuvenated, and at dawn the sun god rose reborn into the sky, symbolizing new life for all. The positioning of the winged sun god above the Osiris emblem was meant to symbolize the rising of the sun out of the netherworld. This pairing of images therefore suggests the dawning of a new day, a metaphor for renewed life.

Lastly, on the wooden board beneath the mummy's feet is painted the galloping pied bull Apis. This was the sacred animal of the creator god Ptah of Memphis. One of its roles was to carry the dead on his back to their tombs, and this explains why it is shown here.

morning. For this reason they are positioned here below his wings. Two snakes, facing the Sons of Horus, represent goddesses who protected the sun god. In the centre of this band is a mummified falcon representing Sokar, a very ancient god associated with the city of Memphis. He was often linked with Ptah and Osiris, to form a composite deity who promoted the resurrection of the dead.

The central image of the lower zone is a fetish, or emblem, which stands for Osiris, the chief god of the netherworld. It is mounted on a pole and is topped by ostrich feathers. The original fetish was kept in the temple of Osiris at Abydos, where it was surrounded by standards

NESPERENNUB'S APPEARANCE:
facial reconstruction

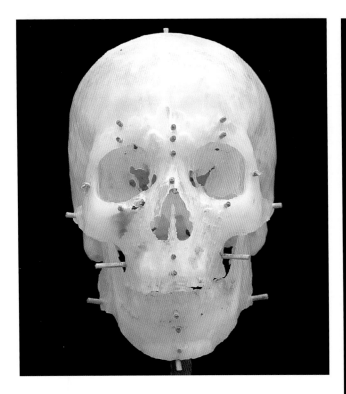

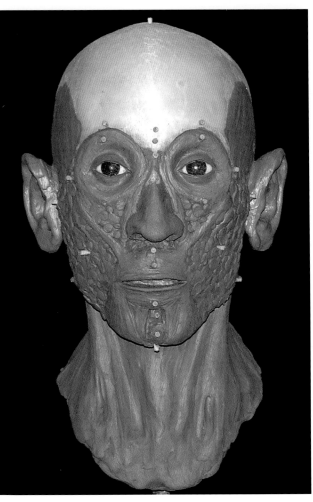

ABOVE LEFT Facsimile of Nesperennub's skull, modelled from CT data. Pegs have been attached to indicate the depth of soft tissue usually present at specific points on the skull.

ABOVE RIGHT Head with muscles, eyes and ears added.

OPPOSITE Nesperennub's probable appearance in life: the finished head, with skin tone and eyebrows added.

USING skulls, it is possible to reconstruct the living appearance of people from the past. Standard techniques for this have been perfected in police work, where it is often necessary to identify decomposed bodies, and the same process can be applied to ancient remains. Pegs are attached to the skull (or to a replica of the skull) at specific points. These indicate the depth of soft tissue usually present at those locations on the human head. With these pegs as reference-points, muscles, eyes and skin are modelled using clay and attached to the skull. When the process is complete, artificial colouring can be applied to the skin and eyes, and hair added to produce a realistic impression. The bone structure, of course, does not determine every contour of the soft tissues, and so a reconstruction of this kind can never be one hundred percent accurate. None the less, it generally provides a recognizable likeness of the individual.

This procedure can even be followed when the skull is physically inaccessible within the wrappings of a mummy. The CT scans are first accessed and the data relating to structures made of bone selected; some manual 'editing' of the data is necessary to remove desiccated skin and other dense materials which could be confused with bone. A stereolithographic replica of the skull is then made in resin.

Nesperennub's skull has features commonly found among ancient Egyptian men. His lower jaw is notably substantial. The reconstruction takes account of his age as estimated from the state of his skeleton, and he is shown without hair, as befitted a priest.

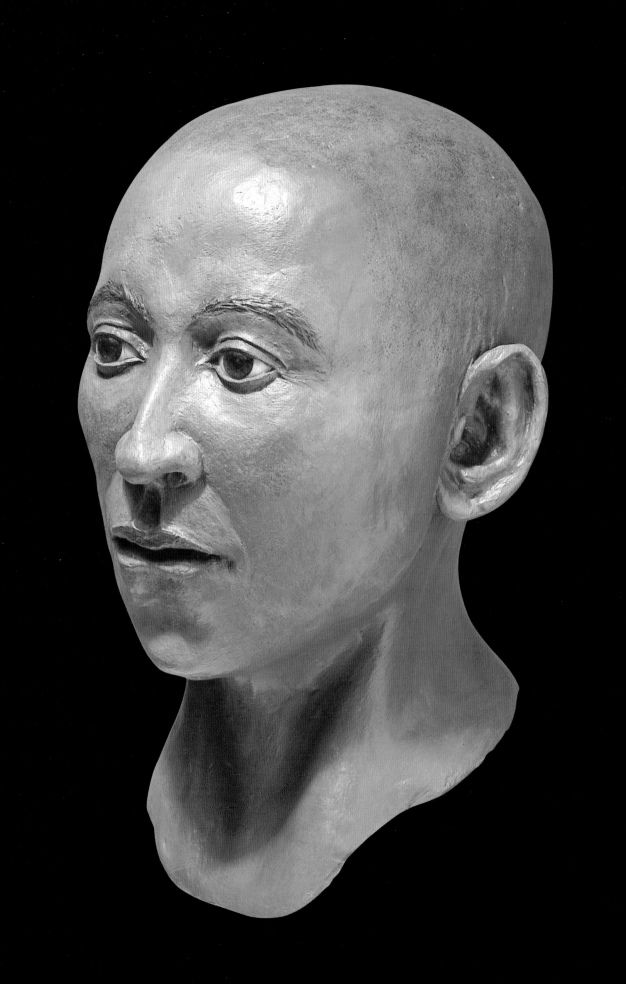

CONCLUSIONS

THROUGH the meeting of the museum world with those of sophisticated medical imaging and computer technology, the secrets of life, death and mummification in ancient Egypt can now be presented to the public in exciting new ways, revealing more than could ever be discovered through unwrapping.

Attitudes to mummies constantly change. Once regarded merely as curiosities, they are now seen as valuable storehouses of knowledge about all aspects of life in ancient societies. At the same time their status as the remains of once-living people has been brought into sharper focus, a factor that must be taken into consideration in their future treatment.

For the scientist and historian, mummies continue to offer the potential to gain crucial new insights into the past, but it must be remembered that they are an exhaustible resource, and the refinement of methods of extracting information non-invasively will play a key role in the next generation of study. CT scanning has already evolved significantly since its inception. The future may also see MRI (magnetic resonance imaging) scanning adapted for use on mummies. On this pathway to knowledge, Nesperennub has unwittingly acted as a pioneer, helping to point the way to new discoveries and new horizons.

Further reading and web resources

Taylor, J. H., *Death and the Afterlife in Ancient Egypt* (London, 2001).

Taylor, J. H., *Egyptian Mummies* (London, 2010).

Dodson, A. and Ikram, S., *The Mummy in Ancient Egypt* (London, 1998).

David, R. (ed), *Egyptian Mummies and Modern Science* (Cambridge, 2008).

Aufderheide, A., *The Scientific Study of Mummies* (Cambridge, 2003).

Gray, P. H. K., and Dawson, W. R., *Catalogue of Egyptian Antiquities in the British Museum*, I. *Mummies and Human Remains* (London, 1968).

The British Museum registration numbers for the individual objects illustrated in this book are listed in the captions. You can find out more about objects in all areas of the British Museum collection on the museum website at britishmuseum.org.

Acknowledgements

University College Hospital London for the use of its radiography facilities, and in particular Fiona Henderson, superintendant radiographer at UCH.

IMA Solutions, in particular Benjamin Moreno and Julien Arrue for the development of the three-dimensional images from the CT data.

Picture credits

All illustrations are © The British Museum, except where stated otherwise.

Andrew Gize, University of Manchester, and Janet Davey, Monash University, Melbourne: p.29 (lower right).

Claire Thorne: drawings pp.48, 54.

John H. Taylor: pp.9 (top), 13 (bottom), 14 (top right).

Map of Thebes p.9 and Plan of the temples of Karnak p.13: based on I. Shaw and P. Nicholson, *British Museum Dictionary of Ancient Egypt* (London, 1995).

Manchester Museum: p.28 (top).

National Hospital for Neurology and Neurosurgery: pp.30 (bottom), 39 (bottom), 47 (bottom).

Phoebe Apperson Hearst Museum of Anthropology and the Regents of the University of California: p.20.

St Thomas' Hospital: p.29 (top right).

University of Manchester: p.60.

View of Thebes p.12 (top left): from S. Aufrere, J.-Cl. Golvin and J.-C. Goyon, *Egypte restituée* (Paris, 1994-7).

Quotations from ancient Egyptian texts, pp.22, 27: from Jan Assmann, *Death and Salvation in Ancient Egypt*, translated by David Lorton (Ithaca and London, 2005), pp. 13, 55, 119.